SUSPENSION PREVENTION

Acknowledgements

This book would not have been possible without the support, encouragement and flat-out hard work of a number of kind and talented people including Lynn Provost my 20+ year business advisor and best friend; my business partner Lesley Hensell who took over my work and hers for weeks at a time so I could complete this book; fellow seller Kelly Loach who encouraged me to start my *Reinstatement* and *Get Clean, Stay Clean* consulting practices and gave me early insight into the process; arbitrage expert Chris Green who always seems surprised when I act on his excellent ideas; my local Amazon seller mastermind group for sharing so many great ideas that made this book better; Cordelia Blake and Jay Bayne of ScannerMonkey for their tremendous support and for welcoming me into their seller community; Tess Castleman for having such incredible faith in me even when I wavered; my mother Jean Sims who dropped everything to help proof and edit my book; and my father Philip Stine, the inspiration behind my first book and the entire concept of helping sellers be better in a Step-by-Step$^{(SM)}$ way.

Dedication

This book exists because my clients shared one of the worst events of their business lives with me. Some were in desperate straits with layoffs and bank workout ("collections") officers getting scary on the phone. These are passionate empire-builders who were shocked to hear Caesar fiddle while their Rome burned. Yet they are also practical, humble people who were willing to make big changes in how they did business in order to stay on the Amazon platform.

Some even said later, "While I'm not glad this happened, I learned a lot. I was making mistakes. I can do better." Moments like these make me admire my clients and make me even more resolved to do everything I can to help them succeed.

I would be understandable for them to walk away from this experience with a broken entrepreneurial spirit – and many of them were temporarily crushed during the process – but the majority of them got back on their feet and kept selling afterward.

My early clients in particular are the reason this book exists today. We were in uncharted waters, and their faith in me led to dozens of sellers being reinstated who had previously been denied or banned.

I have learned as much from my clients as they have learned from me. I am very grateful and happy to dedicate this book to their spirit, chutzpah, work ethic and decency.

I would also like to dedicate this to Tom, my husband of 21 years, and Eric, my son who ate a lot of ramen noodles and pizza while I typed. Tom is the stable rock in our family who lets me be adventurous, try new things and occasionally fail. He has always been my biggest supporter, not only in words but in deeds. He is the nurturer who takes care of all of us - son, wife and dogs. I'm a lucky woman.

Having Eric in my life reminds me what's at stake - his future. I am so grateful for all his help with the business, from lifting boxes to emptying the dishwasher and taking out the trash. "I'm not a slave!" he protests as he does it anyway. Thank you, son. I can count on you, and it means a lot to me.

Tales from the Dark Side of Selling...

Verity Mawkyard[1] read her email in disbelief. Her heart started pounding and her anxiety threatened to consume her. Suspended for selling counterfeit items. How could this be true? She bought everything from retail stores! Her items were New. Two of the items on the list she had, in fact, never even sold before! How could Amazon do this? She was guilty until proven innocent, and it was infuriating. Her integrity was being called into question, and everything she was trying to build was crumbling in those three words: "selling counterfeit items."

George Muzzle watched in horror over the course of a few hours as the rest of his Amazon accounts – U.S., Canada, U.K., and Mexico – disappeared because his France account had been suspended for shipping problems: hundreds of thousands of dollars a month worth of sales were gone for something he thought he had fixed by switching to a new shipping service. Surely Amazon didn't expect everything to be better in a day? Why would they stop his sales on the other platforms where he had such great metrics?

"I've had enough!" said Joly Stick. "Someone's going to pay for this." It was the fourth time he'd been suspended, and he knew exactly what was going on and who was doing it. He'd gotten it resolved before with Amazon, and it infuriated him that there was no institutional memory whatsoever. No one who could say, "Oh wait, we already resolved this issue in Joly's favor." No one who could look at his account and say, "Oh, this is a competitor not a customer." All his competitor had to do was file a

---

1 My thanks to Charles Dickens for creating such awesome fictitious names. That man knew about pain, and you can tell even in how he names things. All names and situations have been changed and mixed up to protect my clients. They've suffered enough.

policy violation, and Joly was suspended again, and again, and again. Not anymore. They messed with the wrong goombah this time.

Betrayal, anger, grief and panic can be overwhelming when you've been suspended. Most of my clients have experienced all these feelings during the process. But Joly and his fellow sellers were not quitters. They had something to fight for, and they came out swinging. They weren't perfect sellers, but they didn't deserve this either. They picked up the phone, and they did something about it. They called us.

Their stories represent only a few of the more than 100 sellers we've helped to fight back in the past year. This book is a view from the trenches, while the war is waging overhead. You are holding the very latest in reinstatement intelligence in your hands – gathered at great emotional cost from our clients. We figured it out the hard way – through experience. Because Amazon won't be clear, direct, logical, reasonable or helpful in any way, you are on your own if you are suspended or banned from the platform.

We think this is a terrible injustice to Amazon's third-party sellers. We think the two-to-three-week backlog they have on responses to some appeals is reprehensible, and the ongoing series of horrific technology "glitches" we have seen them make is scandalous.

Who are we? We are the consulting team at *Online Sales Step by Step*. We are all former business consultants, and three of us have been third-party sellers on Amazon for the past five years. Our founder Cynthia Stine started consulting on the side three years ago to help new FBA sellers get started. Fall 2014 is when she got her first client reinstated ... and then another and then another. Through her work with Joly Stick, she began to realize something was seriously wrong with the suspension process, and that the cards are badly stacked against third-party sellers. It started as a trickle that became a flood of suspended sellers by summer 2015.

Now Cynthia's selling business is on the side, and her consulting practice is full-time. We are growing rapidly to meet the demand. If you need us, we can be found at: http://onlinesalesstepbystep.com. Our hope with this book is that you will never need us for reinstatement services. It was written at a furious pace to try to stem the tide of Amazon account suspensions.

We see it as part of our company goal of *Suspension Prevention*. You may think this battle does not concern you. We assure you it does. No one is too big, too squeaky clean, too tied-in to Amazon to not get caught by the suspension robots. Your best strategy is to be proactive. Forewarned is forearmed.

Amazon doesn't share information, so our conclusions are based on observation and experience. Things change weekly at Amazon in terms of reinstatements. Reinstatements were much faster and more easily accomplished only a few months ago. We will provide updates through our blog.

While all of this sounds scary, take heart! Our success rate is very good. The vast majority of our clients are eventually reinstated. The email from hell is not the final word .... Even when it says it is the final word.

Table of Contents

Introduction

Every day, dozens to hundreds of (mostly) decent sellers get suspended or banned from the Amazon platform worldwide. How do I know that? I'm estimating based on how many of them call me every day. I assume that most of those suspended will write their own appeals, and only a fraction will call me or one of my competitors for help.

In fact, very few Amazon sellers ever call on me when they are first suspended and still have access to the appeal button. I get the texts, emails and calls usually after they've failed their own appeals. At the point they call me, they have been denied (at best) or banned ... even if they don't realize it.

Suspended means you still have a chance to write an appeal. Denied means that appeal was denied but you may still be able to re-submit a revised version of your Plan of Action. Banned is when Amazon sends you the letter telling you that your appeal has failed and they will no longer read your emails. Usually in this email they tell you when you'll get your money back and that it is against Amazon policy for you to open another account.

What my clients realize loud and clear is that they are losing tens of thousands of dollars a day to hundreds of thousands of dollars a week (some of them) during their time away from the platform. They have inventory that isn't turning, employees that they have to layoff, loans that need to be paid ... this is no small matter to most of my clients. They aren't sleeping, they can't work, and they are seriously freaked out. I get desperate texts at 2 a.m., many of which I'm awake for because I'm still writing appeal letters.

That Amazon uses such a blunt cudgel to get a seller's attention is depressing and upsetting to me as a fellow seller. It is not very partner-like, friendly or supportive. The fact that my clients can't talk to someone about their situation is maddening. They are abandoned by their selling partner and treated coldly. They don't understand what they did wrong, and Amazon's suspension letter confuses them. I would, perhaps, feel Amazon was justified if my clients had committed some terrible sin against Amazon or its customers, but 90% of the time that is simply not the case.

Sellers are being suspended because of the rise of the robots at Amazon and the company's culture of "purposeful Darwinism[2]" that regularly culls employees and poorly performing partners. Seller's accounts are being flagged because of keywords and activities by malicious competitors.

Of all the things wrong with suspensions, this is probably the greatest sin by Amazon in my eyes. No seller should have that kind of power over another seller's account. But because everything is automated, anyone who has figured out the system can get another seller kicked off the platform pretty easily. You would not, for example, want to get on my bad side. I have learned how to fight back – something I do regularly for my clients once we get them reinstated.

Suspension by robot is followed by an auto-letter that may or may not have something to do with the actual reason a seller is suspended. What we've learned after more than 100 successful reinstatements (this book was written in summer 2015) is that the suspension letter is usually the tip of the iceberg.

The suspension letter lists ASINs with problems. But another phrase in the letter reveals that this is not the whole story. "Here are **some examples** (my emphasis) of your listings that we believe violate this policy." At that point, they list some ASINs that triggered the robots. Later in the letter, they usually tell you to check your account to see what else you can find. Based on that vague direction, you are now expected to create a Plan of Action that tells Amazon why this problem will never happen again on your account.

I feel especially badly for my clients who went to Facebook or the Amazon seller forums for help first. Most of them are crucified by a seller community that does not understand the new reality. The reason suspensions have jumped so dramatically isn't

---

2 "Inside Amazon: Wrestling Big Ideas in a Bruising Workplace" by Jodi Kantor and David Streitfeld, August 15, 2015. *New York Times.* http://bitly.com/InsideAmazonNYT.

that there are a bunch of shifty sellers finally getting caught (I wish!). Rather, there are good sellers getting caught up in the net designed to catch poor performers.

My clients are often given bad advice by other sellers. These friendly advisors may be sharing information based on their own experience from months to years ago, before the system was so aggressively set to suspend. They are told to write in bullets and keep their plan to less than a page – which would be a disaster for many of my clients. They are told to write form letters rather than letters with specifics. They are told to write Jeff Bezos – a huge mistake if their Plans are not ready. They are told to grovel, plead, lie and/or open new accounts, among other things. They are told that you can't get reinstated unless you know someone on the inside (FALSE). They are told that you can't get reinstated after being banned (NOT true).

They are often told that you only get one suspension so if you are suspended again, you are out. This is not always true either. If you keep getting suspended for the same reason, I suspect it might be true. However, clients that I've reinstated multiple times were suspended for different reasons each time.

These are myths. My clients stand on their feet and tell the truth. We get them reinstated based on their merits, not on lies or tricks. I will show you how we do that in this book. I will dispel some common misunderstandings about suspensions and Plans of Action.

While Amazon has always had suspensions and banned sellers, I trace the rise of the robots back to fall 2014, when Amazon undertook a major upgrade to several of its seller systems including the feedback removal system. I have consulted with Amazon sellers for years about improving their businesses. Fall 2014 is when I started to get suspended clients.

I am tremendously grateful to my early clients. We were in uncharted waters, and we experimented. When something didn't work, we tried again. We learned from every encounter. Persistence won the day. Our Plans got tighter and better. What you hold in your hands is thanks to the patience, faith and trust of dozens of sellers who believed in me.

It is my hope that my clients' stories will inspire, relieve and motivate you. Whatever state your Amazon business is in, it can probably be better. You don't have to be suspended or banned to benefit from this book. In fact, I hope that this book will serve as an early-warning system for my readers. I hope that you never have to call me or my team because instead, you caught problems early and fixed them before Amazon suspended your account.

If you are suspended, I hope this book helps you get reinstated without my help. What?!? Yes. I've done my best with this book to make you successful without me. Despite training five people to help, my backlog is a week as of this writing. It distresses my team that we can't jump on them faster despite working 12+ hour days. We all look at this book as a way to help the simpler suspensions get resolved and to focus our attention on the more complicated, larger cases.

In these pages, I share my approach and mindset. I show you techniques that work and exactly what we think Amazon is looking for in a Plan of Action. For those of you reading the Kindle, Nook or PDF versions of this book, I've hyperlinked as much as possible so you can jump around and read just the parts that interest you. For softcover readers, I created a detailed Table of Contents to help you navigate. I expect parts of this book will become outdated as Amazon changes its approach to suspensions. Already we have seen a slight thawing in their letters to our clients – a bit more helpful, a bit more explanatory and less brusque.

I have created a special Reinstatement Center where I will – among other things – update the book. As Amazon changes policies and approaches, we will keep you apprised so if you should need to write a Plan of Action in the future, you will have information you need to be successful. If you are reading the eBook you already have access to the Reinstatement Center. If you bought the softcover version of this book from Amazon, go to http://suspensionprevention.com/freeupdates to get access.

I've included a glossary of terms at the end, a list of frequently asked questions and a bonus chapter on *Against Amazon Policy* that talks about some of your options if Amazon denies your appeal and bans you from the platform.

Part I

Rise of the Robots

.

1

Rise of the Robots

"How could this happen to me?!?" is the question pretty much all my clients ask me first. Most of my clients are decent, experienced sellers. They've sold for years without a problem and felt secure in their operations. Many of them have excellent performance metrics and are suspended for policy violations that don't even make sense to them. They erroneously believed that suspensions only happen to "bad" sellers who don't care about the customer.

The truth is they've been overtaken by Amazon's automation. If the Skylab envisioned in the "Terminator" movies were to ever come true, Amazon would be ground zero for the robots – not the military. It's ironic. Fanatic about data and process automation, Amazon relies heavily on its various searchbots to identify potential seller problems.

I use "robots" and "searchbots" to describe the algorithms and automatic processes behind suspensions. It is how I visualize the dispassionate and soulless actions in my head. Considering how many Amazonians call themselves "Amabots," the term robots or searchbots is pretty accurate.

My team recently confirmed what we suspected which is that Amazon has raised its standards of what it expects from its sellers. The new algorithm that was implemented earlier in 2015 overwhelmed Amazon's Seller Performance group with how many sellers were suspended. At the time of this writing (August 2015), the average wait time for a response for a product quality suspension is three weeks. This has been confirmed with internal Amazon sources as well as by our own observation.

For those of your fortunate enough not to know what it is, here's the anatomy of a suspension:

1. The robots find metrics they don't like. Sometimes, these are the metrics that you see in your Seller Rating. Sometimes, they are not.
2. Amazon puts your account under review. They may or may not tell you this is going on.
3. Your account is suspended. You get a performance notification. You are offered a chance to appeal.
4. You appeal by writing a detailed Plan of Action. This proactive plan is supposed to explain why the problems happened, and how you will prevent them from happening again.
5. Amazon can accept your appeal, ask questions, deny your appeal or ban your account. If you are banned, it is for life. They will shut down any attempts to open another account. They are very good at detecting new accounts from banned sellers.
6. You can attempt to revise your Plan of Action after being denied or banned, but it gets much harder at this point. Your Plan is put at the bottom of the pile or discarded.

The triggers used by the searchbots scoop up sellers without regard to how long they've sold, how much they sell on the platform, how many problems there actually are with the seller's account or even whether or not the claims are actually true. From what we can tell, you are allowed three "hard hits" to your account in a six-month period, up to five a year before you are suspended. There are also "soft hits" which aren't as concerning to Amazon. You get more of those a year, but we're not sure how many more. Velocity matters. If you have three claims in one day that is worse than three claims in six months. A hard hit might be something like "counterfeit," a soft hit might be something like "not as described." They change what is important to them so something that is a soft hit today might be a hard hit tomorrow.

There is no institutional memory with the searchbots, so a seller who has been approved to sell a specific restricted product may find himself suspended again and again for the same issue he already supposedly resolved.

4

Working with Seller Performance to get reinstated is like working with a goldfish in a bowl – no memory whatsoever. "Look, there's a castle! Look, there's a castle! Look, there's a castle!" the fish says. You not only never get the same person twice to look at your appeal, but they also won't look to see what has already been done or said in regards to your appeal.

No one is monitoring the suspensions to see if the suspension was triggered by a competitor or a legitimate customer complaint. There is no nuance or understanding applied to the situation. "Counterfeit/fake/bootleg/Used instead of New," are all weighted the same in Amazon's world. It doesn't matter that the customer may have said "fake" or "does not match the description" simply to get free shipping on their return.

Sell DVDs that play on foreign players or only in Region 2? You are asking for trouble because your customers won't read the description, and then they'll blame you when they can't turn off the subtitles or when the DVD doesn't play on their player (not to mention the folks who wonder why the DVD doesn't play on their CD player...). I have a client who no longer sells "Borat" DVDs because his customers just won't read the description and see that it is designed to look like a bootleg DVD. That's the joke. But his customers keep turning him in for counterfeit.

Commingle your inventory? You are a suspension waiting to happen – even if you've commingled successfully for years. If your product isn't labeled with your label, you have no defense against policy violations claimed by your customers and competitors.

Competitor change a product picture on your listing? You are in serious trouble. Not only will Amazon not tell you about it when it happens, they'll hold you responsible for it when your customer complains.

These examples are all policy violations. We have plenty of clients who come to us suspended for performance metrics as well. Some are stunned because their metrics look good – all green, many 90-100s. When we dig deeper, however, we see where Amazon is getting its information. Many sellers do not realize that their FBA statistics are measured separately from their merchant-fulfilled stats, for example. They are looking at the FBA stats – looks great! They don't see the MF problems that are sinking them. The good thing about Amazon is that there is a tremendous amount of data about your account waiting for you to discover. The trick is to know where to find it and what it means to you. More on that later.

To get back to the question of *why*, you only need to look at Amazon itself. I write in more detail later about total quality management and how that impacts everything

Amazon does...but they take it to an extreme. According to recent reports, employees are encouraged to report each other for less than stellar performance and can easily rat out a coworker through the – you guessed it – automated internal system. Every year Amazon fires a certain percentage of its workforce as a matter of course. Its executives have to defend their teams and determine who to sacrifice and who to keep.

Given this culture of purposeful Darwinism, it is no surprise that Amazon would apply those principles just as unsparingly and unfeelingly to its third-party sellers. Not only is Amazon culling the bad performers, they are putting everyone on notice that they have to get with the program of continuous improvement. Sellers are asked to write Plans about transgressions they've not even committed yet because Amazon wants them to address the potential problems now, before they occur.

Once the robots are triggered, everything is automated and impersonal. The letter you get from Amazon is auto-generated, for example. I've seen ones where the robots malfunctioned and the client letter had a bunch of errors where the ASINs were supposed to be. We had to go back and BEG Amazon to fix this error so we could see why our client was suspended.

Usually Amazon will give you some examples. Rarely, however, does the performance notification cover *all* the problems Amazon sees in your account. They might talk about counterfeit but not "Does Not Match Listing." This is important because Amazon is expecting you to identify and address ALL the problems in your account.

In the notification letter they send you, there is often a sentence that encourages you to examine your customer feedback, messages, etc., to learn more. What they mean by that is you MUST find out what else is on their mind. If you overlook something, they might ban you without telling you why. We know this because we've come in behind our clients who failed their original appeals, addressed the hidden issues and got them reinstated.

If you miss something and you are lucky, they might give you a notice thanking you for your plan and requesting more information about the perceived problem. I say "perceived problem" because sometimes Amazon has asked our clients for truly bewildering things. For example, one client of mine had a lot of problems with faulty products, claims of counterfeit and more. We did a thorough analysis and created a plan that addressed many issues. We got a notice back asking us to address "inadequate packaging." We were thinking, "what the...?" because nowhere was there any customer complaint about the packaging. It was the product that was the problem.

We wrote up a brief plan addressing how our client would make sure that all his products were adequately packaged and he got reinstated. We were happy in this case that they told us what was on their checklist because it was not listed anywhere else.

My perception of Amazon's Seller Performance team is a (mostly) happy group of minions who work in the Philippines or India. This image is fixed in my mind thanks to those happy yellow MINIONS® boxes Amazon is shipping lately. When they get your Plan of Action they have a few minutes to compare your plan against their checklist. The checklist is created by the robots and has quotes/phrases and statistics from the following sources[3]:

- Messages from your customers
- Negative feedback – whether visible, deleted by Amazon, or struck-through
- Returns reasons
- A-to-Z claims
- Imperfect order report
- Performance notification(s)
- Past policy warnings
- Secret policy violations (usually filed by your competition against you – they don't show up in Seller Central)

The Amazon checklist includes requirements for each part of the plan. Naturally, you have to address the actual reason you were suspended. If they gave you ASINs, give them an explanation for each one. Then you need to demonstrate to Amazon how you will make sure that problem never happens again with any of your other inventory. In other words, it is not good enough to delete an ASIN from your inventory or to say that you will never sell that product again. You have to explain how you plan to avoid that claim from ever happening again.

---

3 This part we know is true based on the few times Amazonians have looked up our clients' accounts for them.

I can hear the screams of anguish now. I mean, how in the world do you stop a customer from selecting the wrong reason for a return or for claiming "Used for New" when they simply don't want to pay to return something? That's covered later.

If you are following along closely, you've noticed that the robots find a keyword, trigger a suspension and then send you an automated letter. Not until you have filed your appeal do you get a *human* to look at your situation closely....except they often don't even then. These workers are generally not business experts and don't understand how a third-party seller operates. They are not entrepreneurial. They don't look at the world the way you do, and they never will. After all, if they were entrepreneurs they probably wouldn't be working for Amazon. They would be selling on Amazon or creating a new platform to beat Amazon.

"This is a horrible nightmare!" thought William Why. Amazon had told him they would reinstate him if he moved his inventory to FBA. That wasn't even reasonable! His company sold 150,000 SKUs every year. Some of his items were large. The FBA fees would be staggering. Amazon would have to build a warehouse just for their business. Every time he tried to explain this, he got the banned letter from Amazon. After years of selling with no serious problems, he faced the stark reality that he needed to tell his 18 employees that they might be out of a job. Even worse, no one at Amazon would talk to him. He couldn't make his case to a human. And then the phone rang. It was Amazon Lending. They were concerned about his $400,000+ loan and his missed payment. Something needed to be done quickly or else the friendly loan officer would be replaced with the unfriendly workout officer.

Ironically, the loan officer – who had something at stake – was the most helpful person William knew at Amazon. He read the Plan of Action and sent it to Seller Performance with a personal note as to why he thought it was a sound plan that made sense. Four days later, William was reinstated.

William Why is a great example of why it would be nice if Amazon's workers *were* business-savvy. He has more than 150,000 SKUs for sale on Amazon.com. Some are hot sellers, and others sell one or two units per year. Some of the items are physically quite large. Any FBA seller understands right away why sending in 150,000 SKUs is bad for Amazon as well as the seller. Yet Amazon told William he would only be reinstated if he sold every item via FBA. We eventually convinced Amazon to accept a compromise (William now sends some small, fast-selling items FBA, but maintains his large MF operation) by breaking down the argument into very simple sentences and by garnering the support of the loan officer.

If your appeal/Plan of Action gets too granular and in the weeds, you've lost your Amazon reviewer. If your Plan of Action blames others, protests your innocence or sucks up to Amazon, you've just wasted valuable time. I don't know how many minutes an Amazon minion is allotted to read your plan and make a decision, but it isn't very long. You can't afford to waste time talking about anything else but how you are going to improve and change things for the better.

This is generally what Amazon experts mean when they say the plan should be short: don't fill it with useless pitching, bitching and moaning. The plan itself needs to be as long as it takes to clearly communicate that you've learned something and that you are changing your behavior for the better. I've had 12+ page plans (single-spaced) when the reinstatement called for it.

Assuming this is your original appeal, the minion reads your plan, compares it to the checklist and makes a decision: approved, approved with caveats, need more information, or denied. You get a form letter stating your status within two days normally, but I've seen it take two weeks or more.

If you get approved with caveats, or denied and submit a revised plan, the process starts all over again with a new minion. The new person goes through the same process of comparing the revised plan to the checklist...assuming that they even read your Plan. They aren't looking at notes from the previous Amazonian, for example, stating "everything is good except the packaging." Doesn't happen. Many of my clients simply get auto-letters telling them they are banned or asking them to address something they already addressed in the Plan. If you get a quick response, in fact, it is most likely that no one read the Plan. It is a robot response.

This is why patience and persistence are required to get reinstated. This is why it can take hours to weeks to get reinstated after the Plan is filed. Amazon is not consistent or predictable when it comes to *their* deadlines. If you have already failed with your first appeal, it will take longer to get someone's attention.

Once you are reinstated, you are not out of the woods. Now, every single time a customer complains of anything, you will get warned. Sometimes you will need to provide invoices or a mini-Plan of Action for that one particular issue. You might even get suspended again. My personal record for a client is four times suspended and reinstated (Joly Stick). I hope Amazon is done with him now.

I tell you this not to scare you, but to prepare you. Forewarned is forearmed. My job for my clients and in this book is to help you navigate your own storm-tossed seas with confidence. Don't take "no" for an answer until you are sure that someone has actually read your Plan. The shorter the return email from Amazon, the less likely your Plan was read.

REINSTATEMENT NOTES:

1. The robots don't care how big you are, how great your other stats are, or how long you've been selling on Amazon.
2. The robots catch a lot of decent sellers in their nets along with the big transgressors.
3. You need to address *all* the issues in your account, not just the ones Amazon mentions in the suspension notification.
4. There is no institutional memory at Amazon. No one is looking over your history and making a thoughtful decision.
5. You aren't out of the woods once you are reinstated.
6. These suspensions are unlikely to stop or get better anytime soon. They are a natural outcome of Amazon's culture of purposeful Darwinism.

2

Not Paying Attention

While the rise of the robots has led to a lot of suspensions, the other side of the equation is seller behavior – or perhaps lack thereof. Many of my clients got suspended because they weren't paying attention. Their customers complained, and they didn't react. The notices that Amazon sent them didn't seem important and they didn't act...or at least not fast enough. They didn't realize that there was anything particularly wrong with their business practices. Not having any benchmarks besides Amazon's desired performance metrics leaves a lot of room for variance, and Amazon hates variance.

I'm as guilty as the next seller for skimming over the zillions of Amazon emails we seem to get every day, and I have a great deal of sympathy for the busy seller trying to get it all done with little help or resources. My clients weren't goofing off, and their neglect was unintentional. It doesn't matter to the Amazon robots, though.

Because they weren't paying attention, my clients are not the best source of information about their own accounts. They don't remember policy warnings or customer complaints. Stuff that is important to Amazon isn't at the top of their minds – especially when they are so heartbroken about being suspended. When we conduct an assessment, we go into their account cold and pull the data that Amazon sees. *Then* we sit down to talk to the client. It helps a lot. Sometimes our clients are as surprised as we are at what we find.

Certain things I've seen in my clients' accounts shocked me. During an assessment, I told one fellow, "I can't believe Amazon didn't suspend you sooner." I'm not normally so blunt, but this person wasn't getting it even when I laid out all the problems in his account. He had what I call an "eBay mentality" on top of everything else.

On eBay, the seller owns the listing and the customer. On Amazon, there is one listing and Amazon owns it and the customer. On eBay, being unique is a good thing. Amazon prizes uniformity and compliance. My sellers who come from eBay are much more proprietary over their customers, listings and inventory than Amazon sellers.

I'm going to irritate good, responsible eBay sellers when I say this, but I've seen a lot of eBay sellers who don't seem to find anything wrong with selling used, shoddy, incomplete, expired and defective products on Amazon. They engage with their customers in a way that Amazon frowns on. Some of the Amazon policy violations that come from what I consider the eBay mentality:

- Products not matching the listings: incomplete games sold as "collectible," products with missing pieces, different colors sold under one color listing, the picture shows something is included that isn't...the list goes on.
- Putting variation information in the seller notes.
- Making a unique listing for every product they sell, instead of placing it under an existing listing.
- Trying to promote their own company brand, website, or phone number on the listing, in your listing notes or slipped into the product package.
- Cute "thank you!" notes stuffed into product packages.
- Selling a knock-off generic electronic under the branded listing.
- Selling samples.
- Including items not on the original listing as "surprises."
- Fighting with the customer over a return or refund.
- Making it hellish to return a product in general.
- 64 A-to-Z claims in 90 days (what the hell?!).
- Uploading badly lit pictures taken on someone's kitchen table without the requisite white background.
- Listings created that don't meet Amazon's standards, from the headline chock-full of keywords that make no sense to the ALL CAP marketing copy, and on and on.
- Plagiarism, copyright infringement and stolen photos from the brand owner.
- Condition problems, where "New" is not really New.
- Ugly and slipshod packaging.

- High rates of product damaged in shipping.
- Generally unprofessional approach to their Amazon business.
- Heavy reliance on USPS.

No matter the size, your Amazon business has to be top-notch or they will kick you off. eBay has room for personalities, quirks and different ways of doing business. Amazon does not.

On-time delivery, excellent customer service, secure product packaging and easy returns seem to be the exception rather than the rule among my clients who started on eBay and moved to Amazon. It gets them in trouble because they don't learn the new rules with Amazon. If you started with eBay, be aware that you have an unconscious bias that could hurt you. You need to read all of Amazon's policies and procedures carefully. Understand the new world order with Amazon, or you won't be selling on Amazon for long. You can find Amazon's policies and procedures in Seller Central "Help" and at the back of this book.

Of course non-eBay sellers have their faulty mindsets, too. Many sellers try to apply brick-and-mortar practices to the online world, for example, and it doesn't work. Amazon is the gold standard in online customer service and needs to be the model we follow, not the customer service model at your local discount store. Here are other examples of seller mistakes I've seen:

- Horrifically rude customer service – brusque, terse, dismissive, condescending, obscene, cutting, callous and sometimes just plain non-existent.
- Treating customers as potential thieves and liars.
- Blaming the customer for product problems.
- Inadequate staffing (owner was handling everything from customer service to shipments on a high-volume account, which is insanity).
- No internal quality-control processes.
- No or insufficient employee training.
- Slow refunds.
- Slow responses to customer inquiries and/or only available during regular work hours.
- Late and slow (more than five days standard) deliveries.

- Selling repackaged returns as New. (Amazon can do that – you can't.)
- Making the customer email you multiple times to get anything done.
- Order-taking business (drop shipping).
- Buying from liquidators and closeout suppliers.
- Buying inventory off the back of a truck and other *really* questionable sources (from a "friend" who could not be bothered to provide receipts or invoices, for example) to resell on Amazon.

Do any of these bullets seem uncomfortably familiar to you? Then fix them now! Don't wait until Amazon suspends or bans you. You don't have to wait for Amazon to suspend or ban you to have an internal Plan of Improvement.

Rosetta Dust wore her suspension like a thorny crown. After 17 years selling on eBay and five on Amazon, busting her butt every day to ship out orders, deal with customers and pay her mortgage, it might be over. Two bitchy customers had basically done her in. She was sick to death of dealing with entitled customers who wanted to rip her off at every turn and who had so much power over her account. It felt like blackmail and took all the fun out of selling. It was the same at eBay. She seemed to spend all her time dealing with unscrupulous buyers on both platforms as well as fending off Amazon who was poaching her suppliers and undercutting her prices…she really couldn't decide which platform was worse.

She took it personally and couldn't clear her head. She couldn't see that she had made some mistakes. Her perception was that Amazon was suspending her so they could steal more business from her while she was suspended.

In the case of cross-platform seller Rosetta Dust, she needed to get out of the customer service business altogether. It was eating her up and not helping her. Her suspension basically reflected her frustrations with the business – her anger was showing up in violations. After she was reinstated, we switched her to Amazon's automated customer service and worked with her to create her first FBA shipment.

She has an uphill battle because she also needs to re-think her inventory and to stop selling so many small-margin items where part of her profit is in the USPS shipping fee. This is part of the eBay mentality that she needs to shed. She needs to learn about pricing higher when you sell FBA and how to compete differently than she's competed for nearly two decades.

These dramatic changes are happening because selling is how she supports herself. This is not a part-time gig for Rosetta. The suspension pushed her (albeit unwillingly) in a new direction.

Besides the poor seller behaviors, I've seen some really beautiful accounts where you could tell the seller was on top of everything, attentive and responsive. In fact, it was a struggle to find anything wrong in their accounts. In most cases, these sellers were willing to make changes and to learn. Constant improvement was a habit they already possessed, and their accounts and long histories of happy customers showed it. These guys got caught up by the robots sniffing around for counterfeit and other policy violations.

I want to emphasize again that not paying attention is not the same as lazy or careless. I had one client who boasted in her original appeal how much her company's customer service had improved and how they had fixed problems from the past. When I went through her account, I found example after example of unhappy customers not being taken care of by the customer service team, mistakes made by the shipping guys with sending the wrong inventory to customers and so on. A lot of internal business processes needed to be fixed right away.

She was stunned and asked me, "Where did you get this? Where did this come from?" I then showed her the reports that I'd pulled from her account. She had no idea. I felt badly for her employees because I knew she was furious – at them, at herself for not knowing...you know how that goes. Now she checks those reports every week. She is holding her team to a different yardstick, and it is working. Her stats are improving. Her customer complaints have dropped significantly.

Another client knew he was getting returns for a certain product he sold, but he didn't realize just how many nor that they were such a high percentage of his total returns. By looking at the returns report, he is now able to see alarming trends and stop selling faulty product before the volume triggers the robots.

As much as I dislike the way Amazon suspends seller accounts, I have to admit that the robots often *do* uncover real problems. Like canaries in the coal mine, metrics such as a high number of A-to-Z claims, frequent returns, customer complaints, seller cancellations and slow customer response are warning signs that there is fundamentally something wrong.

By compiling all the isolated problems, we are often able to discern the systemic issues underneath that are causing them. We will talk with our clients about how their businesses work and how they handle things now, to try to figure out what the problem is and then how to fix it. That fix becomes a key part of our Plan of Action. This is why so many appeal letters to Amazon fail, no matter how nicely written, they do not address the underlying issue that is triggering the robots. If the sellers don't fix that/those problems, they will be suspended again in a few weeks or months.

The solutions don't have to be hard or huge, though. One company that had a high number of returns on a product was able to significantly reduce returns simply by adding a special email to their Feedback Genius customer feedback program. The SKU-specific email provided a PDF of simplified installation directions and "frequently asked questions" that greatly reduced the need for customers to return the product. It gave customers a one-click way to reach my client before sending the product back. We added this email process to the Plan, implemented it after they were reinstated, and saw immediate results.

If you are not familiar with the program, Feedback Genius helps sellers solve customer service problems through strategic, targeted emails. It integrates with your Amazon account to send the emails through the platform. Most of my clients send two emails – one the day the product is delivered and one a few days later asking for Feedback. Because of the way the emails are written and because of the easy links to get help, return products, etc., Feedback Genius significantly increases positive feedback while reducing negative feedback.

By using Feedback Genius, sellers often see their positive review rates of 1%-3% bounce up to 8%-10% overnight. ASIN-specific emails help my clients address particular problems. Whenever I see an ASIN with a high number of returns, I always think about how Feedback Genius might reduce that problem for my clients.

Another client that was getting a high number of negative feedbacks from customers for late deliveries realized that Amazon's delivery estimator was not working for European customers. We changed the settings on his Feedback Genius to eliminate foreign customers from the "out for delivery" email (which relies on Amazon tracking data). Complaints dropped immediately because customers were no longer getting inaccurate delivery information.

I don't mean this to be an ad for Feedback Genius. We use a lot of tools and ideas to help our customers. These examples were so fast, simple and effective, I had to include them. The thought process in getting a seller reinstated requires an understanding of business processes, knowledge of Amazon tools and problem-solving. This is why I turn away potential clients who just want me to look at their Plans. I am not a simple letter writer, and it would be a disservice to them to not know what else might be going on in their account. The Plan of Action is the end result of analysis and problem-solving between me and the client.

Now that our clients have actionable data, they get busy cleaning house and fixing broken processes. They re-examine everything. Sometimes they have to fix broken processes before we can submit their Plan of Action. We report on their results and help them put their Plans into steps that Amazon's minions understand. I had one client who had so many things wrong with his account, I despaired that Amazon would read his 12-page single-spaced Plan of Action, let alone reinstate him. And yet they did. They saw how thoroughly he had examined his mistakes and the very real changes he was making in his company, so they gave him another chance.

Another client who owed Amazon money from a loan sent his Plan to the loan workout officer to show that they were working hard to get reinstated. The officer responded that this was one of the best plans he'd ever read, and that he reads a lot of them in his job. He sent the Plan to contacts of his inside Seller Performance and urged them to reinstate my client, which they did.

This has been our experience over and over again with Amazon. If we can get a human to read the Plan (not easy after someone is banned), Amazon will often give them another chance. I've seen Amazon forgive heinous transgressions when they could see meaningful changes taking place and it was clear that the seller learned something from the process. To me this indicates that Amazon does want a partnership with its third-party sellers.

REINSTATEMENT NOTES:

1. Paying attention means reviewing your account regularly.
2. If any of those account problems I listed seem all-too familiar, fix them now.
3. Many suspensions reveal systemic problems in a seller's organization – look at your processes.
4. Fixes can be simple once your end goal is clear.
5. Amazon will forgive a lot if they can see that you've learned what happened and made real changes.

Performance Notifications – Achilles Heel of Merchant Sellers

I rarely see Amazon FBA sellers suspended for performance issues unless they also merchant-fulfill some items. The turnaround and delivery dates it demands makes being an Amazon merchant expensive, so you need a crackerjack shipping team. If I were into conspiracy theories, I would speculate that Amazon wants everyone to sell FBA and is deliberately putting the squeeze on its MF sellers to get them to switch. Several of our clients have moved all or part of their inventory to FBA in an effort to get Amazon to let them sell again. It usually works when the issues are related to delivery.

A performance violation almost always means that a seller is not meeting Amazon's suggested metrics for delivery of their products to the customers or that they are not properly servicing Amazon's customers. Yes, I said *Amazon's* customers. All sales on the platform belong to Amazon, and they are very particular in how their customers are treated. Performance suspensions usually involve one or several of the following issues:

- Order Defect Rate (ODR) greater than 1%
- Negative Feedback rate greater than 6%
- Contact Response Time more than 24 hours
- A-to-Z Claims
- Late shipments
- Lost packages

- No tracking information
- Seller-cancelled orders
- High returns (higher than 3% in most categories)
- Too many items damaged in shipping
- Slow response to customers' requests for refunds
- Slow to stop selling faulty products
- Slow to act upon previous performance notifications

This isn't necessarily a complete list, but it is a list of the most common reasons sellers get suspended for performance. Nearly all of these can be instantly resolved by switching to FBA. We've noticed that Amazon makes it harder and harder for merchant-fulfilled sellers to be successful on its platform. Today's requirements are more stringent than just a few months ago. If you think things have changed, you are right. Not realizing that fact has caught many sellers by surprise. For example, when you loaded up to Amazon the tracking information for a package, it used to count as "shipped." Today it doesn't count as shipped until the *carrier* scans in the tracking information. Overnight, sellers were dinged for late shipments that used to be on time. Many MF sellers saw their stats take a nosedive even though their business practices hadn't changed.

Here's a more detailed look at what Amazon means by these terms:

Order Defect Rate Greater Than 1%: The order defect rate (ODR) is made up of several metrics including Negative Feedback, A-to-Z Claims, Contact Response Time, Refunds, Seller-Cancelled Orders and whether or not the customer contacted you about their order for any reason. They call these "imperfect orders." You can download your imperfect orders report for the past 90 days and see what Amazon sees when it looks at your account. [See "Reports" chapter.]

I pull the data into a spreadsheet. Depending on how you sort it, you can see which ASINs are getting the most imperfect orders and why. You can also quickly see what kind of dings you are getting, which is the first step towards reducing your imperfect orders. If a significant portion of your Order Defect Rate is due to late orders, you address that differently than slow contact response time.

One thing to keep in mind: even if your ODR is lower than 1%, that doesn't mean your stats are actually good. You can still get suspended for too many A-to-Z claims, too many returns or too many negative feedbacks for a particular ASIN, for example. That's why it is important to look at each metric closely.

In addition, Amazon keeps your metrics for FBA and MF separate. If you are one of those sellers who fulfills some of their own orders and uses FBA for the rest, you might get fooled by your seemingly great numbers and not realize they are for FBA and not MF. Your MF numbers may be awful. In fact the less you merchant fulfill, the more likely your numbers will be awful simply because you don't have the volume of sales to off-set a negative feedback, A-to-Z claim, etc., for an MF order.

Here's an example of a seller (me) with Mary Poppins FBA scores ("...*practically perfect in every way!*") but lousy MF metrics. I've made three sales in the past five years MF. One of them was returned.

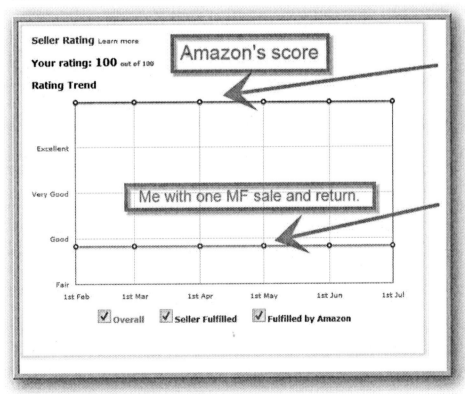

I'm an FBA seller. These few sales are anomalies. For a seller with a lot of MF items, however, this chart may be the only sign they have that something is wrong. Once you know you've got problems, you can pull up MF reports and find out what is going on. If you are relying on the green check marks (or lack thereof) to tell you when there is something wrong, you'll get caught by surprise as so many of our clients did.

Lastly, your ODR is calculated over time. Even if you work quickly to improve your stats, your rate will creep up slowly over weeks. This will impact your ability to get the Buy Box, among other things. For example, I had one client who couldn't get the Buy Box for weeks after his reinstatement, even though he had the lowest price and even though he had quickly removed a lot of negative feedback that was bringing down his ODR. After about a month, his ODR had improved enough that he started to be eligible for the Buy Box again.

Negative Feedback Rate Greater Than 6%: When you look at your feedback rate in your performance pages, you are generally looking at your *positive feedback rate*. I want you to look at the flip side, which is your negative feedback rate. If your positive feedback rate is 93%, that means your negative and neutral feedback rate is 7%. Experience has shown us that Amazon wants your negative feedback rate to be 3% or less (97% positive). You will get the Buy Box more often and customers will feel more comfortable buying from you.

Amazon separates neutral feedback (3) from negative feedback (2 or 1), but I have no idea why the impact of a 3 on your account is negative just like a 2 or 1. And just to make it more confusing, 3s are really hard to remove. You have to basically prove to Amazon that the customer actually meant the comment to be positive if you want the 3 to be removed.

Amazon won't suspend you solely for negative feedback until you drop to 90% positive. Then you are in the danger zone. If you've just dropped into the danger zone, don't panic. Amazon gives you a week or so to fix the problem with the customer. I've dropped below 90% before and was back up to 97% or higher in a few days because I got the feedback removed.

For newer and/or smaller sellers, it doesn't take very many negative feedbacks to drop you low. This is why you need positive feedback – lots and lots of positive feedback. Besides getting rid of negative feedback, I have my clients start a campaign to solicit more positive feedback.

I tell my clients to contest every single negative feedback for the previous year. Because sellers can't use the automated system while suspended, I have them start with a fairly recent select group of unhappy customers and work with them by email to get the feedback removed. That way, we can show progress in our plan. Sometimes, if the feedback is obviously a product review or includes cursing, we call Amazon Seller Support and ask them to strike the feedback. I got a review with the word "crap" in it removed once because I claimed I was offended. Getting even a few negative feedbacks removed can make a huge difference. Once you are reinstated, you can use the automated system to get rid of many more.

When using the automated system, I tell my clients to contest all of the feedback, even the ones they wouldn't normally. Why? Because the robots work in your favor with this one. There is some kind of algorithm at work with the automated feedback system that automatically approves the removal of a lot of negative feedback. I've gotten feedback removed for my client that was very old. If you are denied, make a case for it and try to get it approved through your case log. You have nothing to lose and everything to gain by trying.

Negative feedback happens to all sellers regardless of fulfillment method, of course. What makes negative feedback particularly problematic is that Amazon's searchbots scour all those feedbacks and use them as the basis for policy violations, among other things...even if you had that feedback removed. This, I think, is so unfair that there isn't a word big enough to describe it.

We discovered this with a client who had three negative feedbacks – none of which were related to the policy violation mentioned by Amazon – and thousands of positive feedbacks. In this particular case, the client had an account manager inside Amazon (our client has been selling for many years on Amazon – starting back when you were assigned an account manager) who unofficially pulled up the stats on her account. The reasons given for the violation were all from negative feedbacks our client had had successfully removed in the past. We hadn't looked at those because we thought they were gone forever.

Since that day, we've combed through our clients' feedback reports and looked at those that have been removed as well as current negative feedbacks. This is part of why it takes us so long to conduct an assessment. We have to read several months' worth of customer messages and feedbacks to ferret out account problems, plus at least a year's worth of performance notifications. [You would be surprised at how many of our clients forget to tell us they were suspended previously.]

Contact Response Time Greater Than 24 Hours: Amazon wants all customers to get answers in fewer than 24 hours – preferably less than 8 hours on average. That's why slow responses cost you so much in terms of points against your ODR. If you are suspended, you can't afford even one late response.

I tell my clients they have to check and respond to customer inquiries at least twice a day during the week and once a day on weekends and holidays. The easiest way to do it is to get the Amazon Seller app downloaded to your phone. You can adjust the settings in such a way that a message will pop up on your screen when you have a buyer message, and you can address it immediately. Obviously, if you get dozens every day, you'll want to have a team that handles these. Amazon's message center lets you create templates that you can use for common customer situations like "How do I get a refund?" "When is my package arriving?" and other standard inquiries like these. You or your team should be able to answer most inquiries quickly.

Miriam Denial didn't know what the big deal was about customer complaints – they were Amazon's problem. That's why she used FBA, so she wouldn't have to deal with customers. But now it was a problem because they wouldn't let her back on the platform. They chastised her like a child in the email telling her "despite repeated warnings...." What warnings?! This was a dreadful shock. Miriam didn't even know where to begin to create this "Plan of Action" they wanted to see.

Because I'm 100% FBA, I rarely get customer messages. Most go directly to Amazon to deal with their issues. *However* please note that if a customer contacts you, you MUST respond! I've seen FBA sellers get in trouble for contact response time because they erroneously believed they were not required to answer inquiries. They thought Amazon would do it for them. It is OK to direct a customer back to Amazon to get a refund or return, but you still need to answer them in a timely way.

One more thing – don't cheat! I've seen sellers who automatically click every customer message as "no response needed." (One hopes they go back later and take care of the customer.) This is against Amazon policy and if they feel you are overusing this feature, you get a stern warning from them. They want you to respond to your customer in a timely way, not just click a box.

A-to-Z Claims: A customer files an A-to-Z claim either when they can't get satisfaction from you, or when they don't realize they should have contacted you first. Basically, they are unhappy and want fast action. A surprising number of my clients did not realize how seriously Amazon takes A-to-Z claims. These are considered severe problems and, ideally, you would have zero claims. Zero. How is that possible when customers file the claims in the first place? Simple. Jump in as soon as a claim is made and refund the customer.

What?!? I can hear the gasps from here. Yes. You need to refund their money and move on. If you let Amazon close that A-to-Z claim, it will hurt you a lot more than the money for the refund. By acting quickly, Amazon won't count it against you. You can still protest/appeal with Amazon and tell your side of the story. If you really believe that the claim filed by the customer is bogus and you are going to protest it, make sure you don't do it too often. In MOST cases, Amazon decides in favor of the customer and takes the money out of your account for a refund anyway. You might as well do it yourself and spare the hit on your ODR.

Just because you plan to refund the person doesn't mean you can't ask for the product back. Be aware that if they get impatient for the refund, however, you could suffer. For items that did not cost me much out-of-pocket like books, or items that can't be re-sold, like food, I tell the customer to keep the item, and I give them an immediate refund.

If it is an expensive and/or resellable item, send them a pre-paid shipping label to return it. Let them know you will refund them the moment the item is scanned and you can see it's on the way back to you. Often the customer will tell *you* when the package has been collected. You can also keep an eye out for the tracking number and quickly make a refund when it appears. This should satisfy Amazon and the customer. Whether or not you want to take the cost of shipping out of their refund is up to you. If they've filed an A-to-Z claim, I'd eat the cost of the shipping, personally. You want them to be happy and to withdraw their A-to-Z claim.

For all of you out there who exclusively sell through FBA, you probably have no idea what an A-to-Z claim is. Amazon doesn't allow A-to-Z claims on FBA items. It is not because you are such an awesome seller. Sorry.

When I'm working with an MF seller, I often look at the A-to-Z claims first. They tell me a lot about that seller. If I see a seller with a lot of claims, I know they have other problems to deal with inside their organizations. A-to-Z claims are the canary in the Amazon coal mine. They indicate poor customer service, shoddy packing, slow shipping and delivery of products, drop shipping (often) or short-sighted return policies. These problems have to be fixed, or the seller will just get suspended again down the road.

Late Shipments, Lost Packages, No Tracking Information: These tend to be related problems. Late shipments may indicate poor processes at my client's facilities and/or an inability to handle the number of orders they are getting every day. If I see a client with a lot of lost packages, late deliveries and unreliable tracking information, I tell them, "stop using USPS." Seriously, the post office is terrible about deliveries and should not be used for your Amazon business if you are having any complaints about shipping – even though Amazon uses USPS.

A short-term adjustment is to change the handling times for your problem ASINs that aren't getting delivered on time. That will help some, but most people don't read the shipping times when they buy a product. If your adjusted times are outside the customer's expectations, they will still complain.

This makes my clients unhappy when I suggest it, but the fact is that although the USPS has tracking barcodes, etc., they are poorly used by postal workers. It is not uncommon for the post office tracking system to say a package is in transit long after it has been delivered. If a customer claims not to have gotten a package, there is no recourse for them besides going to the local post office to see if it is still there. This is absurd, and it makes a lot of customers really unhappy. They don't want to hear from my clients that they really have no idea what happened to their package and to take it up with the USPS. If you are going to use USPS, then you better be prepared to FedEx overnight a certain number of replacement orders. I've not run the numbers myself, but it seems that even a few express replacements a month begin to make more reliable carriers like UPS® seem affordable.

UK sellers have similar problems with the Royal Mail®. Sellers in the UK use the Royal Mail a lot because most packages are delivered within a day or two at the most without paying expedited fees. The UK is comparatively small, and it doesn't really make sense to use priority or express mail for most items. However, the Royal Mail loses packages, too. When I suggest to my clients that they pay for tracking to cut down on customer complaints, they all tell me, "No one uses tracking with the Royal Mail." I answer, "Amazon does." Don't be penny-wise and pound-foolish on this issue. If you are getting delivery complaints, change what you are doing.

Another tracking problem I've seen is with international orders. A high percentage of my clients who sell on international platforms do so MF from the United States. This astonishes me. I can immediately predict what I will see in their account: unhappy customers who had to wait too long to get their items, a high volume of damaged products in shipping, problems with customs, problems with tracking and delivery, and lost items.

If you are going to fulfill your own inventory to Europe, go with DHL®, UPS or some other reliable international carrier with tracking that will deliver your item directly to the customer. Don't make them go to customs to pick up a $30 item. Don't use some cheapie carrier whose tracking stops at the country's borders where the item is turned over to a local delivery carrier (like the Royal Mail). Don't deliver to countries that are known to be rife with corruption and graft. You'll lose your shirt and garner a lot of negative feedback.

Sometimes the problem can't be solved with another carrier. The seller needs to sell FBA in that country or give up that marketplace. My clients sometimes resist or are unhappy about this reality. In some cases, my clients explain that they wouldn't be able to make their margins if they sold FBA. When I show them how they can actually charge more, they sometimes change their tune. In other cases, they can't raise their prices and they need to change their product mix instead. For example, a client who was selling nail polish and other cosmetic items had a problem because there was no margin in any of his products for FBA or a better carrier (like DHL). I suggested he sell more expensive items with better margins. Why work himself to death for nail polish? Why lose his selling privileges over something so small? Almost all his negative feedback was around delivery. If he couldn't compete charging more for reliable shipping, then he should sell something else.

Some clients are resistant to FBA overseas because they are afraid of VAT. They don't know how to set it up, and they don't want to learn something new. When their problems are all performance-related, I insist they use FBA for some of their more troublesome SKUs and see what happens to their complaints.

Seller-Cancelled Orders: This is where the seller cancels the order, not the buyer. Seller cancelled orders are a huge indicator of drop shipping problems. The seller cancels an order because she doesn't have the item she just sold on hand. She tries to place an order with her drop shipper, who is out of stock as well. This is a huge reason why Amazon does not like drop shipping. While they cannot stop you from doing it, they can penalize you every time it doesn't work out right. In fact, drop shipping from an online retailer (like Target.com) is against Amazon policy and they will suspend you for that. You can still drop ship from a manufacturer. I've had clients argue with me that their partners are reliable, that drop shipping is great, etc. I then point out that they are suspended because their partners aren't reliable, and they can't afford one more cancelled order. Amazon has ZERO tolerance for cancelled orders. I've had sellers suspended for this reason alone.

Most sellers who drop ship are cheap and don't want to actually buy inventory until they've pre-sold it. It sounds great on paper. It works poorly on Amazon. Sellers are completely at the mercy of another company both to have product and then to deliver it to the customer in a timely way without breakage or other quality problems. It is a recipe for disaster. I tell them to purchase some of their better-selling items and either keep them on hand for self-fulfillment or send them to Amazon FBA.

Another reason I've seen a lot of seller-cancelled orders occurred when a buyer asked the seller to cancel the order for them. My client didn't realize it was being counted against them. They thought they were helping a customer. I taught them how to show customers where to cancel their own orders. That way, they could spare themselves the unnecessary hit to their metrics. Amazon only gives buyers an hour or so to cancel an order. If your customer is contacting you outside the allowed time for a cancellation, don't do it for them.

High Returns: Amazon won't give you a target metric for returns, but our experience indicates that they prefer 3% or less in most categories. Clothing and shoes tend to have higher returns and Amazon appears to accept that fact. Generally what Amazon is looking for are patterns. Do you have one ASIN with a lot of returns as a percentage of overall sales? That points to a faulty product. If you have a lot of returns in a category or family of products, it might indicate an education or listing problem. It could be a manufacturing problem.

For example, two clients had high-volume returns on replacement garage door openers and vehicle luggage racks. These were category-specific rather than brand- or ASIN-specific returns. The problem was that customers didn't know how to make the products work and then returned them as faulty. By adding information (like dimensions) to the listings, providing revised instructions and more support before and after the product was delivered, both clients were able to significantly reduce their returns across the board.

Damaged in Shipping: If Amazon fulfills your orders, damage in shipping is their problem. This holds true *except* if Amazon determines that poor packaging on your part is leading to poor delivery on their part. Then they expect you to fix the problem. I've only seen this once. Most often what we see is merchants fulfilling orders that are getting smashed during delivery. This goes back to what I said earlier about working with a reliable carrier.

Damage in shipping can also be another indicator to Amazon of drop shipping. If you are not fulfilling your own orders, you have no control over how the final product arrives to your customer. If you are getting delivery complaints and you know it is from a particular drop shipper, you need to stop working with that company immediately.

What particularly gets Amazon's goat is when sellers seem not to be paying attention. One of my clients had a lot of complaints about broken glass items and glasses...a LOT. And yet he did nothing about it. He sent out replacements to unhappy customers, but he never fixed the underlying problem, which was that the glasses were poorly packed for transit. When I pointed out that all the glass should be wrapped in bubble wrap of some kind, my client argued that it would be expensive in terms of manpower and supplies. "Then stop selling glass," I said.

In our Plan for clients with these complaints, we tell Amazon that our clients will be watching their reports carefully and will quickly stop selling an ASIN that has a certain number of complaints of broken product until the packaging issue can be fixed. That usually does the trick. Amazon isn't unreasonable. They know that some things get damaged in shipping. What triggers the robots is when there are multiples, and it seems like the client isn't paying attention. The volume of sales for an item will often dictate when the panic button is pushed.

Slow, Slow, Slow: One of the things Amazon hates to see about performance issues is...nothing. Inaction or slow action by the seller triggers the robots all the time. I can't tell you which straw will break the camel's back, but I can tell you that if you are not addressing problems quickly as they come up, you will be suspended.

I've seen clients argue with their customers about refunds, drag out the process over weeks, and then wonder why they had so many A-to-Z claims and/or negative feedbacks. Customers' demands for refunds (and not receiving refunds fast enough) are one of the most consistent reasons I've seen for suspensions. In this way, we sellers need to be a lot more like Amazon.

Clients are also penalized for responding slowly if they are selling a faulty product. If you are getting a high number of returns or complaints about a product, you should stop selling it until you can figure out exactly what is going on. To continue selling it is madness. Yet I've seen clients doing just that many times. Either my client did not realize just how many returns there were, or he just thought of returns as the cost of doing business. I tell my clients that if they see *three* complaints about an ASIN they need to investigate and possibly suspend their listing.

They are aghast. "Do you know how many of those I sell a week?!" they ask. The robots don't care. I turn it around on them and ask, "How many SKUs are you actively selling?" Usually there are hundreds to thousands of them. "How many of them are perfect day after day, week after week?" Usually most of them are. "Oh! So there are only a few ASINs that have returns? Then maybe you should look at that." It begins to dawn on them that Amazon wants *all* their orders to be perfect. Then they think Amazon is being unreasonable and they complain about that.

If I am able to get them to dig in and actually find out why a customer returned a product, they are often shocked to find out the product was actually faulty or damaged in shipping. It wasn't just buyers trying to get free return shipping. It actually was a problem they could fix for their customer.

If you are looking at your reports regularly, you can catch problems before they escalate to Amazon's attention. What you *should* see in your returns report and imperfect orders reports are a smattering of claims evenly across many ASINs: a damaged product here, a return there. That's normal. If you see certain ASINs hogging the limelight, there's a problem. I follow a "three strikes and you're out" rule. If you have three defective or "Not as Described" claims in a short amount of time (say a month) then there's something wrong.

Slow responses to Amazon policy warnings and notices also get sellers suspended. For most performance violations, you get one warning email, and then you're suspended. The suspension could come within hours or a couple of days of getting the warning. The original notice often says that you don't need to respond. I disagree. I think you should investigate the claim and respond to Amazon with the results. This way you'll have it on record, should you be suspended, that you took action immediately and determined the source of the complaint.

By the time you get the warning, it can be too late to avoid suspension. That's why I strongly urge my clients to review their reports often and thoroughly. Try to catch issues before they come to Amazon's attention.

In the "Reports" chapter, I go over in detail every report that you need to monitor regularly to stay out of trouble with Amazon.

REINSTATEMENT NOTES:

1. MF sellers are the most vulnerable to performance-related suspensions.
2. Amazon scours your negative feedback, customer messages and returns reports for complaints.
3. Drop shipping puts you at the mercy of another company's business practices, product quality and delivery relationships.
4. Work with reliable carriers – if you are getting complaints, your carrier is not reliable.
5. Swift refunds disarm most A-to-Z complainers.
6. If you have more than two refunds and/or defective claims for a particular ASIN or category of products, stop selling them until you can fix the problem.

4

Policy Violations

Performance problems are easier to fix than policy violations for the simple reason that you can improve on performance. Your progress is measurable. Policy violations are like IRS audits – you are guilty until proven innocent. The robots scan through your account, and if they find a trigger keyword or a combination of keywords, you are suspended. It is unclear how many signs they need to declare a policy violation. I've seen as few as one and as many as 10 or more before Amazon shut someone down. In addition, the keywords that triggered the violation often have little to do with an actual policy violation.

There is no consideration for all the time you've sold without any problems. In Amazon's world, all policy violations are bad.

Amazon is treating us like it treats its own people – combative and in-your-face. You have to fight to stay in the game no matter your past with them. To make the situation even more galling, you can't just say, "I won't do it again or in the future." You have to create a Plan that shows how you will make sure it never happens again in the future...even though it has never happened on your account in the first place! It is this level of indignity that drives my clients crazy, and I can't blame them.

Stephen Marquick thought he was doing great on Amazon.com. A young guy with a lot of ambition, he dreamed of having a big business that shipped across the world. When he first looked at his notice, he didn't take it very seriously. They were wrong about the whole "does not match listing" thing. He would just tell them so, and the problem would be fixed. He checked out the Facebook groups, wrote a short and snappy appeal explaining his items matched the listings ... and he was banned in less than two hours.

When you are hit with a policy violation, it is critical to get to the bottom of the claim. You need to find the specific claim(s) that triggered the robots, so you know how to write your Plan. When the minions pull up your Plan of Action, they are going to look at it against the actual keywords/messages from the customers. It is part of the checklist.

If you write something generic about always buying from legitimate sources, and the actual complaint was "not as described," or "damaged in shipping," you might have a problem getting reinstated. We have seen a lot of failed appeals and one of the mistakes we see a lot is that the seller was using a generic Plan of Action they found on the internet or a short bulleted plan without enough detail. Because the Plan was not specific as to what was actually happening in the seller's account, he/she was denied.

Amazon wants you to explain the ASINs it gives you and any others you find in your own research that violate policy. It wants to see a Plan that clearly explains how the problem will be avoided in the future.

A quick distinction: There are account suspensions and listing suspensions. Amazon suspends individual listings all the time for various reasons and some of them can be the same as you see in an account suspension, like counterfeit. You may have to go through the same steps to get your listing reinstated as you did for your entire account. Listing suspensions *can* lead to account suspensions. Even if you get reinstated on the listing, we often see the same ASIN listed as part of the account suspension later.

This is not good news, I realize, but it does show the importance of staying on top of every policy warning and suspended listing you get from Amazon. At least for my clients who get suspended later, we can show that they were reinstated for that listing previously and re-supply the proof. It makes the process go faster. Usually an *account* suspension involves multiple ASINs, not just the previously suspended one. From Amazon's perspective, you may not have learned the lesson from the listing suspension. You addressed their complaint for one ASIN but didn't look at all your ASINs. Disproving counterfeit for one item, for example, is NOT the same as showing Amazon that counterfeit will never happen on your account.

VIOLATIONS

Counterfeit: While this suspension notice says your products are inauthentic and/ or fake, the reality is often very different. We've found, for example, that counterfeit can mean "Not as Described," or it could mean that the packaging is different from the picture. (We see this a lot with cosmetics.) It could mean that a customer used the words "fake," "bootleg," "counterfeit," "false" or "bogus" somewhere in their message or negative feedback. One seller had a customer who specifically said, "I don't think it is fake but it seems like it might be used instead of new." The seller got suspended for counterfeit.

Counterfeit claims are addressed two ways. First, you have to provide invoices showing the ASINs in question are legitimate and New. This is true even if the complaint isn't really counterfeit. You must comply with Amazon's request for invoices. The invoices must have the name of the product and UPC code (if possible), date of purchase and quantities. Often with a counterfeit claim, Amazon wants to see invoice quantities that will cover your past 180 days of sales. If you sold 100 units in the last 180 days, your invoices need to show at least 100 units purchased.

What's that, you say? You bought your products at Marshall's, a thrift store, a liquidator or a dollar store? You have a problem. Your receipts won't have enough detail, and they'll be denied. Sometimes, you can promise to never sell the item again and delete it from your inventory. Amazon might reinstate you. Often they won't. We have helped our clients come up with solutions that Amazon found acceptable. I'm not trying to be coy here, but some strategies are best not made public.

Invoices are step one. Step two is to figure out what really happened to trigger the robots and to try and fix that problem. DVDs, CDs, supplements, electronics and baby formula (go figure) are highly susceptible to counterfeit claims. One of my clients had to stop selling a discontinued (but not expired) shampoo because of the high number of counterfeit claims by customers. Shampoo! It was crazy.

In similar situations, I often say to my clients, "How much is this product worth to you?" If it is worth a lot, then we fight for it. If not, drop it from your inventory. Let's say that the problem is outer retail packaging. This happens all the time, when a manufacturer creates new packaging for the product but the UPC and product inside is the same. In this case, the seller needs to:

1. Prepare a picture to add to the listing that shows the new packaging – NOT replace the main picture, but add a secondary picture.
2. Prove to Amazon that the alternate packaging is legit. Usually the manufacturer's website is sufficient.
3. Add to the listing (once reinstated) that the product comes in multiple packages and to see pictures for possible variations. You may not be able to change the listing depending on who created the original one.

Electronics are often accused of being counterfeit when, in fact, they are faulty. Some of my clients who buy from liquidators learn to their chagrin that the liquidators often sold them returned and repackaged products as New. Naturally, these returns and repackages are NOT New and many were originally returned to the retail store (where the liquidator buys its merchandise) because they are faulty. In this case, we explain to Amazon that the products are faulty, not counterfeit, stop selling them and recall all units (if they are FBA) for inspection. Obviously MF sellers can just go to their warehouse for inspections.

Another situation where we see counterfeit claims that aren't really counterfeit are bulk repackages. I've seen this with food, baby formula, cosmetics and supplements in particular. The client buys in bulk and then parcels out the product into one-pound bags or special boxes and bags. The problem is the product is not in the expected retail packaging, so the customer thinks it is fake. This is really a "does not match description" problem, not counterfeit. The client needs to create a new listing for their product that shows it in the plastic bag, plain box or whatever the new packaging is. "No one will buy my product if I do that!" they scream. Well...those are the rules. Sorry.

As a side note, Amazon has created new rules about food repackages that make it virtually impossible for most sellers to repackage bulk foods (like candy and nuts) into smaller portions. If you sell food, be sure to read up on these new rules. There are a lot of steps you have to comply with now including city, state and federal food handling regulations and guidelines.

I had one client who was selling nail polish that wasn't in the retail box. He pointed out that the picture on Amazon showed the nail polish by itself and not in a box. I explained that his customers were obviously expecting something different than what they got – that's why they were complaining and he was suspended. He originally explained to Amazon's satisfaction that he was buying in bulk (like nail salons do), and that his nail polish wasn't in boxes but was legit. He had invoices to prove it. Amazon agreed with him the first time. When he continued to get complaints, they suspended him. He hadn't really fixed the problem.

Another client was getting claims of counterfeit because her lotions and creams weren't in a box. That was the way they were sold in the retail store where she bought the items – there is no box. Plus, she had several customers claim that their jars were half empty and incomplete. We told her to shrink wrap her naked items in the future.

Damage in shipping causes a lot of counterfeit claims, especially if the product is delivered dirty, scuffed or otherwise looking really worn and sad. It may technically be New, but it if looks like it has been sitting under a heat lamp for a week, you get counterfeit claims (among others). An easy fix if you have a product that has a lot of damaged shipments is to pack the product better before you send it to Amazon (if FBA) or before you ship it to a customer. One seller told me very solemnly that the kind of extra packaging I was talking about would be expensive. Equally solemnly, I pointed out that being suspended for counterfeit is also very expensive.

One jewelry seller had a counterfeit claim on a cloth watchband. The problem was that the manufacturer was sending the watchbands in bulk, and not in individual packaging. My client would then put each watchband in a polybag. While the invoices cleared up the counterfeit claim, to fix the problem my client called the manufacturer to see if they had any branded bags or packaging that he could use. They agreed to send him a supply of bags with their label on it and to ship all future product already pre-packaged in the bag with the branded label. He had only to ask.

As a side note, I will mention that the power of relationships is critical. Sellers who have good relationships with their suppliers are much easier to reinstate than those that don't. One client was suspended for a shampoo and seemed very reluctant to give Amazon the manufacturer's contact information so they could verify the invoice. It took me a while to figure it out, but heart of the matter was that the manufacturer forbade its retailers and distributors from selling the product online. My client had bought the product through another business and changed the invoices. He knew that asking for the manufacturer's help would tell them that he was improperly selling their product, which was probably the idea behind the policy violation in the first place. I strongly suspect the manufacturer filed the claim in order to find out the real name of the seller who was violating their agreement.

Another client was able to go to her supplier and have them sign off on a statement supporting her claim of when and where she had bought the product; that it was New and that the UPC code on Amazon for that item matched their internal product code (which was on the original receipt). It made the difference.

I could go on and on about counterfeit permutations. I will address evil competitors and their claims of counterfeit in a separate chapter (Chapter 5). They are a special case, obviously. The bottom line on counterfeit is to find out what is really going on so you can fix the problem and write a Plan of Action that matches what is actually happening in your account.

Product Does Not Match Description: This policy violation covers a wide range of problems. The simplest form is that your product does not match the listing description. This can happen if there has been a picture change, for example. Amazon doesn't send out notices when a listing picture changes, only when the description changes. This catches a lot of people unawares. I had a recent situation with a diaper bag where another seller kept taking down my picture and putting up another. Since these bags were sold with the same UPC codes, we were both right. Anyway, one of the first things I suggest my clients do is to look at the pictures of the ASINs in question. It might well be that the pictures have changed.

The "does not match" problem shows up a lot in negative feedback. Customers who leave seller feedback are asked if the product arrived on time and if it matched the description. They will often choose "no," because the product was damaged in shipping or was late. They may have tried to get a return/refund and didn't get a response from the seller. Or they simply may want free shipping back to you or Amazon. We have successfully defended against this violation by carefully examining and explaining to Amazon what was behind all the "does not match" claims and what our client was going to do about it in the future.

With "does not match," there are usually multiple claims for an ASIN, so it is important to look carefully at the issue. Why are so many negative feedbacks/returns showing up for this ASIN in the first place? If it is because of items damaged in shipping, then you need to fix the shipping problem. If it is a listing problem, either fix the listing or create a new one. Sometimes it is best to buy a UPC code and create your own listing.

We see a lot of "does not match" and counterfeit/inauthentic claims for private label products. It is really annoying. Some sellers will buy a generic product – like a sweater de-fuzz machine – add something meaningless like a sticker and call it a private label product. The only difference may be that the other seller's product same is branded. Then the other seller will defend the product by claiming your product is inauthentic and doesn't match the listing. You are missing the sticker, the brand name or whatever. One client got in trouble because his foot reflexology kit didn't have the foot chart that the other seller had created and added to theirs. It was the same kit. The other seller was sending a separate PDF to customers (by email) with the chart. My client didn't read the listing closely enough when he listed against it, *and* the other seller was improperly offering the foot chart as a PDF rather than with the product. Since our focus was reinstatement, we left the issue of the "improper use of the platform" violation by the other seller for another time.

While the sweater de-fuzzer example flies directly in the face of Amazon's policy of having one listing for a product, the fact is Amazon sees these as separate products.

You need to buy a UPC code and create your own listing – the de-fuzzer without the sticker. I'm not exaggerating. It really is that stupid.

Sometimes the problem is something you add to the product. A gentleman who sold DVDs imported them to the UK from a European country. The DVDs were in English, but they often had subtitles. Customers would complain about this because they did not know how to turn off the subtitles. In an effort to be helpful, he put a sticker on each DVD that explained how to turn off the subtitles and how to contact him if they had questions. This was a no-no on two levels because you are not allowed to lead customers away from the Amazon platform or to promote yourself in any way. And, of course, his product did not match the description.

He kept telling me that his items matched the description exactly, and he couldn't understand it. I kept asking questions until he casually mentioned the sticker and the subtitles. While it distressed me to tell him he had to recall thousands of DVDs and re-move that sticker, I was relieved that we'd figured out the problem. Certainly Amazon was no help. Once he removed the stickers, Amazon reinstated him. We were able to accomplish the same goal (telling customers how to remove subtitles) through emails on Amazon's platform.

Used Sold as New: This is the hot policy violation of the day at Amazon.com right now (summer 2015). We almost never saw it before the end of July, and then suddenly everyone was getting accused of it. This is Amazon's latest tactic to get sell-ers to stop using liquidators and buying from retailers. Liquidators are notorious for selling Used as New. They buy a retailer's remaining inventory of something, which often includes shelf-pulls, returns and repackaged items. It might be the store that did the repackaging or the liquidator, but the end result is that you are selling pre-opened inventory as New. Even worse, a lot of that inventory is faulty. It was returned for a reason.

One of my clients was caught by this recently. A customer complained that his product was used because there was a Circuit City receipt shrink wrapped inside the case. That is more common than you might think, because a lot of people who are returning items stuff the receipt inside the box or container so they don't lose it before they can get back to the store. You can't really expect the minimum-wage stocker op-erating the shrink wrap machine to be diligent about removing it either.

In case you aren't sure what I just said, Amazon does not like retail arbitrage. We found out from an internal source that items bought in retail stores are considered Used by Amazon and "should" be sold as Used. This is for the same reason as the liquidators. Walmart, Target and other retailers often repackage their returns and put them on the shelves. In addition, the distribution chain is broken when you buy a product in a store. It is New to you, but not New when you re-sell it to someone else. Unlike a distributor or wholesaler, Amazon cannot rely on you to be a reputable link in the distribution chain. I said "should" up there because I cannot find anywhere in Seller Central where buying from retailers is expressly forbidden.

As someone who wrote a book about how sellers can get started selling on Amazon with retail arbitrage, this revelation by our source was a real shock. A few of our clients have had to pledge to either no longer purchase from retail stores or to list these items as Used before they can get reinstated. For FBA sellers, this means recalling their products and reconditioning them.

Other items that might be considered Used sold as New include bottled products without a vacuum/safety seal. Amazon policy for FBA dictates that these products must be sealed to prevent spillage and messes. What also happens, however, is that customers think the lack of a seal means the product is Used. If it is not filled to the brim with product, they are sure they got ripped off. It does no good to protest that the item is sold by weight, or that you buy it directly from the manufacturer. The customer does not care, and a polybag isn't enough, either.

For my clients who choose to sell unsealed product, I suggest a shrink wrap machine to keep the lids firmly on the bottle. Several of my clients confessed to using tape to seal the lids. It only made the situation worse as customers were sure that this was used product and that the seller was trying to fool them.

Another client who sold specialty candles had the same issue. Her customers expected a retail box, even though the candle was not sold that way in stores. They claimed her products were Used sold as New. She ended up shrink wrapping her candles so her customer had that packaged experience they wanted.

Copyright Infringement: This violation can be legitimate or related to "does not match." A legitimate copyright infringement claim usually comes with a lawyer and an email from Amazon that encourages you to contact the rights-holder for more details. The email and, sometimes, phone number of the rights-holder is usually in the email. Some sellers erroneously ignore this violation. They decide not to sell on the listing and don't contact the rights-holder. This can get them in trouble because it is unresolved. I've rarely seen a seller suspended *solely* for copyright infringement unless there are multiple offenses, there were multiple warnings, or there were other problems with the account. Still, it is best not to leave it unattended.

Copyright infringement can be simple. In one case, the rights-holder was upset by the use of its picture on Amazon.com. When the client took her own picture and removed the original one, the problem was solved. One time all they wanted was for the registered trademark to be used with their brand name. It was a matter of minutes to update the listing. In another case, the rights-holder was claiming that sellers on the listing did not have permission to sell the product. My client *was* an authorized reseller. By talking to the rights-holder he was able to quickly clear up the problem and get back to selling.

If you resolve the issue with the rights-holder, you need to make sure the agent informs Amazon. Rights-holders have a special email they use to tell Amazon the results of their copyright infringement campaign. Once they send that email to Amazon, you should be reinstated quickly. Your Plan simply states that you resolved the issue and explains your process to avoid future copyright-infringement claims.

What if you can't resolve the issue? In that case, it is especially important that you inform the rights-holder that you have deleted the listing from your inventory and will no longer sell their product on Amazon.com. Once Amazon is informed, you should be able to get reinstated.

OK, now the really tough one: What if you disagree vehemently with the rights-holder and think she is bamboozling Amazon? What if you think the counterfeit claim is really a competitor trying to keep you off the listing? You are probably right. See more about this in my *Dirty Tricks* chapter. For the immediate short term, you are suspended. She is not. Amazon is not going to get involved and mediate this dispute.

If you want to start selling again, you need to get the rights-holder to inform Amazon of your compliance. I realize this is NOT what you want to hear. Once you are reinstated, you are in a stronger position to make your case with Amazon. You may wish to create a new listing with your own brand. (Note: you cannot do this if you are, in fact, selling *their* branded product. This only works for generic products.)

Sometimes competitors will purchase your product and claim to Amazon that it violates copyright because it doesn't include their brand or secret sauce. This is really a violation for "incomplete product" or "Not as Described," but it shows up as copyright infringement because Amazon is not consistent.

You see this with private label products. The competitor doesn't have an attorney zealously protecting his rights all over the internet; he is just protecting his listing. He files the claim through the policy violation email system on Seller Central, so you never see it.

Forbidden/Restricted Products: Forbidden products cannot be sold on the platform, period. Restricted products can be sold if you have permission either from Amazon – as in gated categories – or the manufacturer. While we don't see it very often, suspensions for forbidden products happen. For example, the rules are different in England on the UK platform than in the US. One seller was suspended for selling dog collars with spiked prongs (among other things). These are considered cruel and unusual punishment in the UK and are illegal, not just on Amazon, but throughout the kingdom. This was a case of drop shipping gone haywire. Our client had uploaded thousands of items directly from his supplier's catalog without checking them against Amazon's policies. He had multiple infractions, which is why Amazon shut him down, but it was really just one mistake.

Expired Items: This applies primarily to food, supplements, vitamins, health, and beauty items. Amazon policy is to pull items from the warehouse 50 days before expiration. Some FBA sellers mistakenly believe that Amazon will automatically do this for them. Sometimes they do, but you can't count on it. You are responsible for keeping track of the expiration dates of your products.

If you are an MF seller, you are not obligated to stop selling 50 days before expiration, but you are taking a big risk – especially if your item is of sufficient quantity that it might take the typical person months to use it. Supplements sellers need to take that into account when setting the "stop selling" date on their products. If it is a 90-day supply, it would be wise to stop selling it 90 days + 50 days or 140 days before expiration. Baby formula sellers need to give themselves a bigger window and not only consider the number of servings, but also the fact that Moms are really uptight about formula. They don't want to be even close to expiration. Two to three months, plus the estimated number of days' supply, is suggested.

Clients who have gotten in trouble with claims of expired were selling too close to expiration in most cases – or even selling expired items. Also, sometimes food goes bad before its time. It may get overheated in the warehouse and have its texture change. A normally sealed product might become unsealed, and then the contents are not fresh. If you get multiple complaints about a product being stale or expired, **suspend your listing and fix the problem**. I'm always shocked at the sellers who keep selling a product with 10, 20 or more expired or stale complaints. They should have stopped after two.

For most people, having a spreadsheet or some kind of tracking tool is enough to fix the problem going forward. With other sellers, the problem was so egregious that we had to have a serious talk about business practices.

Manipulating the Platform: We've seen this policy violation a couple of times. This is where the seller is using the platform in an unapproved way. In one situation, the seller had a side-business helping other sellers get approved in gated categories. Amazon came down hard on this seller. She had one warning and then was banned – not suspended –a few days later. This was a really harsh response, and my client didn't have enough time to rectify the situation.

There are other ways to manipulate the platform as well, including some of the dirty tricks explained in Chapter 5. Basically, if you are using the platform in a way that Amazon does not like, they will shut you down. This can be anything from improper emails, paying for product reviews to misuse of Amazon's shipping and more.

I had a client once that was using Feedback Genius in a non-approved way. His company was sending lots of emails to its customers telling them about new products, offering them buy-one-get-one incentives, and reminding them it was time to re-order. My client sold supplements and had a really slick marketing campaign going on. *However,* this is considered spam in Amazon's world. Here I was trying to get the company reinstated for a different complaint and desperately hoping that Amazon didn't have "spam" or "manipulating the platform" on its secret checklist. Once I explained he was violating a policy, my client stopped the behavior immediately.

REINSTATEMENT NOTES:

1. When it comes to policy violations, you are guilty until proven innocent in Amazon's world.
2. Many claims are not as they appear. "Counterfeit" can mean the product got damaged in shipping.
3. "Does not match description" is ubiquitous and can apply to almost any time the customer had an expectation that wasn't met – no matter how unfair this may be to sellers. Counterfeit, defective product, product damaged in shipping...the list goes on and on.
4. When you get more than two complaints of a policy violation, stop selling that item until you can fix the problem.
5. You must get to the bottom of the claim first, before you can write your Plan.
6. Boilerplate letters rarely do the trick in an appeal to Amazon because they often don't address the real issue.

5

It Was The Evil Seller!

"The only thing necessary for the triumph of evil is for good men to do nothing."

—EDMUND BURKE

Ever feel like someone is out to get you? You may be right. I've seen so many dirty tricks played on our clients this past year by other sellers that I sometimes lose my faith in humanity. What's worse is we can't say to Amazon, "the evil seller did it!" or "she's/he's a liar!" to get our clients reinstated. After they are reinstated is another story, but first we have to get them reinstated without being able to tell the whole story.

When a charge is bogus, it is hard to come up with a solution to fix it. My clients are furious when they realize the charges are deliberate. How do you fight back against an accuser you can't see or reach? It doesn't help that Amazon's default position is that you are guilty until proven innocent.

After hours of reading her Amazon reports and looking for reasons for her suspension, Susan Goloring had a huge headache. There was nothing in her account to explain it. No customer complaints, no returns, no negative feedback. Amazon wouldn't talk to her even though she had an account manager. At first she thought she was paranoid, but the idea kept crossing her mind. Could a competitor be behind this? She didn't even know where to begin to write her appeal. She couldn't believe that someone would be so malicious as to do something like this on purpose, and yet ...

In Susan's case it was true. It was tough to write her Plan because she had done nothing wrong. The complaint was bogus and a competitor filed it. We had to write without sounding defensive or accusatory. Our Plan was basically created for an unlikely future. She was a pragmatist and cared more about selling than being right. After she was reinstated, we identified the competitor and asked Amazon for its help to make sure the competitor did not keep filing bogus claims. It has been several months now with no new accusations from the competitor.

Getting another seller suspended is the ultimate dirty trick, and it is reprehensible. Some of these "tricks" may strike you as legitimate seller behavior (changing ASINs, updating listings), so I want to clarify that this is about *intent* and *purpose*. These are not honorable disputes and disagreements among sellers.

While this chapter is about dirty tricks, I must point out that the vast majority of our clients have things wrong with their accounts or business practices that made them vulnerable. This is one of the sources of their impotent rage – if they'd known, they would have protected themselves. The goal of this chapter is to help you recognize your own vulnerabilities now, while you can still do something about it. Once you are suspended, it is much harder to combat your enemy. Make no mistake about it: you have **enemies**, not just competitors. There are sellers who wish you harm, and who will act on it.

A personal bee in my bonnet is the passivity of many sellers toward evil tricks. They think that if it hasn't happened to them yet, it won't in the future. As a collective group, we – the good sellers – need to condemn this behavior and fight these guys. When one of them brags on Facebook about the latest trick they've played, you need to say something and shut down that conversation. One day it WILL be you who is the victim of a dirty trick, if it hasn't happened to you already.

To this end, I am collecting names. If there is a buyer on your account behaving suspiciously, send an email with their name and what you see going on to evilseller@ onlinesalesstepbystep.com. Feel free to include screenshots and pictures. If we happen to see a name pop up on more than one seller account, we can help all affected sellers take action to get them warned off. You are not powerless. We have already done this successfully and will continue to do it until the bad guys stop behaving badly.

Hello,

We are writing because you may have violated our policies by purchasing items from a seller on Amazon.com with the sole intent of closing the listings.

Per our policies, buying an item for any reason other than a genuine attempt to acquire the item at the stated price is prohibited.

Note that failure to comply with our policies may result in the closure of your Amazon.com account.

Thank you for your cooperation in this important matter.

Regards,

Seller Performance Team
Amazon.com
http://www.amazon.com

See a loudmouth on Facebook fomenting bad behavior? Please screen capture and send to me! I'll add to my list and share with Amazon if he/she is *also* a loudmouth on another seller's account. Obviously posting on Facebook is not the same as acting to bring down a seller, so we need proof.

OK, that is the end of my soapbox. Time to get dirty. Here are the most common dirty tricks that we see in sellers' accounts and how to address them:

TRICK: *ASIN change*. This is a simple one where a seller will change an ASIN and hope that no one else notices or protests it. This trick works best where there aren't very many sellers on an ASIN. This seller may add or remove a quantity or add an item like "Bonus Foot Reflexology Chart!" that they know no one else has. Their customers get the new addition, the other sellers' customers don't, and unhappy customers file "Not as Described" claims or even "counterfeit."

All those weight changes you see? Those are sellers trying to make a product impossible for their competitors to make money. That gorgeous gardening coffee table book that was three pounds when you bought it is now less than a pound, with a smaller shipping allowance to boot.

SOLUTION: *Protest ASIN Changes.* When Amazon sends you the list of ASIN changes (I get them daily), look at it and see if you agree. If you don't, then dispute it. When another seller is changing the title or description, I automatically choose to dispute it (click the link in the email from Amazon). This takes me to a page where I can see the full details and decide if the change makes sense or not. I have thousands of books in my inventory, so I see an unbelievable amount of editorial tinkering. Seriously, write your own book instead. It will cure you of ever wanting to re-write a book description again. This is not evil, though, and I usually don't bother to protest.

Weight changes are more serious. I'm FBA. Most of the time, they don't affect me personally because they are in Books which has set shipping and handling fees. For other categories, a weight increase can cause the FBA handling fee to go up which impacts my profitability on an item.

YOU NEED TO KNOW: Protesting an ASIN change is not enough. If this change negatively impacts you, you need to follow up and see if the change goes through. If it does, you are now selling a product that does not match the description any more. You are in trouble.

I had a client recently who was attempting to get a listing fixed that was incorrect. He filed his case with Seller Central. Guess what he forgot? He forgot to suspend his listing. He sold a unit and even though his product was technically correct – the listing was wrong – Amazon sided with the unhappy customer and suspended him from the listing. Now he has to go through the same Plan of Action process as any suspended seller to win back the right to sell that product on Amazon.

TRICK: *Picture change.* This one is really insidious because Amazon doesn't inform other sellers when there is a picture change. I think this is wrong and unfair because an evil seller can really wreak havoc with this. Most of the time when my clients have a picture change (new product packaging, etc.), I tell them to *add* it to the listing as a secondary photo, rather than change the primary picture. This is less likely to get them into a war with another seller, and it makes the listing more accurate.

Manufacturers change their packaging all the time, so there can legitimately be different boxes of product for sale that have the same UPC code and the same product inside. The best way to handle this is to add to the description about the new packaging and to add a picture. You will need to go through Amazon to do this properly because they'll want to see proof that there are multiple boxes/packages for the same product.

Until your picture is added to the listing, however, do NOT list. You will get counterfeit and "Not as Described" complaints. It is not worth it.

Another time I see pictures being changed up a lot is when a UPC is distributed to retailers with variations. This is a retail arbitrage "gotcha" for the most part. I had this happen lately with a diaper bag. The same UPC code belonged to four diaper bags. My competitor kept changing the picture (three times) rather than *adding* to the listing. I got an unhappy customer who wanted the red one in the picture rather than the gray one. This annoyed me since I was the one who created the listing in the first place. The first time it happened, I called Seller Central. I pointed out to them that I had created the listing, and they reinstated my picture immediately. The seller changed it again. I protested again. When the other seller changed it again (WHY does Amazon let this happen?!?), I recalled my product, bought a UPC code, and created a new listing with my gray bags. I relabeled and sent them back in.

This is a particularly irritating trick because there's really no valid reason I can use against the other seller. Their UPC code *is* correct, just as mine is. I should have created the listing with variations (or the other seller could have)...except I didn't know there were variations. I just bought a bunch of gray diaper bags from a store. I didn't have a picture of the red one. This never happens to wholesale buyers.

I could have added variations after I realized what had happened, but I didn't want to get into a prolonged battle if this was an evil seller as I suspected. With my own UPC code and listing, I figured I would likely have the monopoly on the gray bags (most sellers would be scanning the manufacturer's UPC code and getting my competitor's red bag) until I sold out. I would not have to deal with the other seller messing around with the listing on me.

Lastly, the most evil form of this trick is to switch the picture out with something completely different. Whereas my diaper bag scenario is the result of honorable sellers disagreeing, this other situation is not. This is the evil seller who changes a black stuffed hippo doll into a white stuffed dog. The picture doesn't match the description at all, and the innocent hippo seller is the one who gets in trouble. I discovered this trick the way most sellers do: a customer complained. Where was the white dog they saw in the picture? What was this black hippo? Naturally they returned my hippo immediately. Hmm.

Should I mention that this toy had a ranking of over 300,000 in toys? I was planning to sell it over Christmas. The chances of someone buying it before the holidays were small. Oh, and I was the only seller. I bet my competitor thought she/he was pretty smart until I filed a policy violation. Amazon records *every* change on their platform. They know who is changing the pictures. This trick will only work once if the victim fights back. As the victim, you may not ever see who it is. (Many of them create an MF listing and then delete it after the picture is changed.). But rest assured, Amazon knows.

SOLUTION: A lot of good sellers get in trouble from this trick. If you start seeing "does not match description," "not as advertised," or similar complaints from your customers – check it out *immediately*. Go to the listing on Amazon and make sure your product matches *exactly*. Suspend your listing until you can be sure that your product matches the description. When you initially join a listing, be sure to look at the picture and read every word of the description. Check to see if the "Pack of 2" graphic is superimposed on the photo. See the listing the way your customer does. Don't solely rely on the UPC code. If you rely on a listing program as I do, this is incredibly tedious, but it is the only way to be SURE that when you started selling on the listing your product matched. Otherwise, how do you know? Maybe you made the mistake.

YOU NEED TO KNOW: The best way to protect yourself from this trick is to pay attention to negative feedback and messages from your customers and respond quickly. Suspend your listing and find out what happened. If the picture change is egregious and clearly a trick, file a policy violation. Here are instructions in case you need them:

1. Go to "Help" in Seller Central.
2. Choose "Contact Us."

3. Click on "Selling on Amazon" issue.
4. Select "Other Issues."
5. Under "Report a violation" type in the ASIN and your complaint.

You don't need to accuse any particular competitor on the listing, just explain the situation and ask Amazon to investigate for you. If you are pretty sure you know who the competitor is and want to include that information you can, but I suggest you word it politely like, "It seems like competitor X might be the company making these changes based on XYZ that I observed, but I don't know for sure – can you look into it for me?"

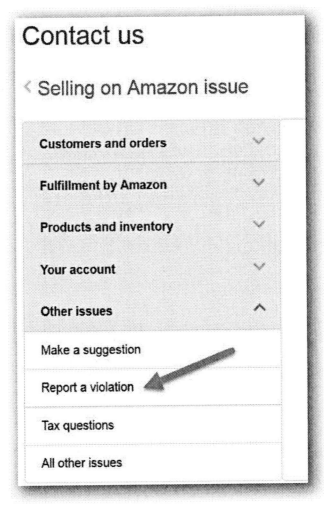

TRICK: *Category Change.* This one trick spawned several "category ungating" services that formed to help sellers defeat this tactic. Your competitor who is approved in a gated category may try to move your product into that gated category on the theory that this would eliminate you from selling because you are not approved in that category. This trick is now mostly played by sellers who are stupid because:

- If you were already selling on the listing before it was moved, Amazon generally lets you stay on the listing, thus defeating the evil sellers' purpose.
- Amazon frowns on this behavior and will come down on the evil seller with a warning or suspension for playing this trick. They want things in the right categories.
- Amazon has tightened its rules about category changes and makes it harder to make these kinds of changes without someone at Amazon approving them first.

I had a bag of Halloween candy that an evil seller attempted to put into menswear and claim was a tie. They changed the title and everything to trick Amazon. You cannot make up stuff like this! Naturally, Amazon sided with me and fixed the listing back, but I couldn't imagine how they had done it in the first place.

Another more successful variation of this trick is to create a new listing in the gated category to sell your product. If you are the first to the marketplace with the latest *As Seen on TV!* gadget and get it into a gated category, you can keep some other sellers from jumping on the listing...at least until someone complains and petitions to move the listing to where it belongs.

It works well if there is some category ambiguity, too. Children's Halloween costumes, for example, are supposed to be in Toys. That's Amazon policy. Sellers list them in apparel all the time, either out of ignorance or cunning. Amazon will move it to the right category for you; it just takes a while. You see the same thing with backpacks (Should they go in office supplies? Luggage? Toys? Sports and Outdoors?), lunchboxes and more. That is also why you will see multiple listings for the same product. All of this is against Amazon policy, and they are working to clean up the marketplace. Their solution is to merge multiple ASINs into one, which makes everybody unhappy.

SOLUTION: Open a case and be patient. If someone has done this deliberately (turning candy into a tie, for example), let Amazon know what you suspect. If it is ambiguous (like backpacks), make your case and point to the manufacturer's website. How do they treat their product? Is it a toy? If there are multiple ASINs, make your case for them to be merged into one in the category you think is best. Amazon won't always agree with you.

WHAT YOU NEED TO KNOW: You won't always win. It is work opening all these cases and hoping you get someone experienced enough to see what you are talking about. Only do it for items where you have inventory quantity, obviously. We had hundreds of bags of candy. We weren't going to take the menswear thing lying down (another seller joined me in the protest).

TRICK: *False Claims in Negative Feedback or Buyer Messages.* Your competitor buys your product and then leaves you a negative feedback screaming, "FAKE!" "BOGUS!" "BOOTLEG!" and "COUNTERFEIT!" They type in large letters so the Amazon robots are suitably impressed with their vehemence. Actually, the robots don't care. They are triggered by the words. You get warned and then suspended almost immediately. The all-caps treatment is often the sign of a competitor who takes joy in their nastiness.

Real buyers don't care quite that much usually. They want their money back. They typically make a case, rather than screaming at the seller. They may be indignant, but they don't often get hostile until they have a problem getting their money back. Many buyers who genuinely suspect counterfeit send you a message first through email explaining why they think it is bootleg. Most decent people don't threaten you and try to blackmail you unless you are giving them a hassle about getting their money back.

Amazon scours your account for keywords, so it doesn't matter if the customer complains in email or through a seller review. From the evil seller's point of view, however, leaving a negative seller review is the icing on the cake. They can ding your seller metrics at the same time as they trigger the robots.

One of my clients sells candles that he buys from directly from manufacturers' retail stores, for example. At the store, no one questions that these are legit candles. Through the mail, however, is another story. Because they were not in a retail box or lid-sealed, customers thought they were smelling a fake. Some even claimed the candles were "expired" or old even though they had only been on the market for four months.

We tried several things to inform customers ahead of time. We changed the listing; we sent special emails when the product was delivered. It helped some, but not enough. Eventually my client started shrink wrapping all the candles which helped the most. The point is, very few of his customers resorted to ALL CAPS or nastiness even when they were unhappy. My client took good care of them and got all the feedback removed.

Another fishy sign besides all caps is the use of *Amazon Speak*. Real people don't talk like Amazonians. When they complain, they use the words they are familiar with and use every day. Third-party sellers use *Amazon Speak*. First, they want to make sure to use the words that trigger the robots. Second, they almost can't help it. As sellers we're unconsciously brainwashed by all the messages from Amazon that we read. I'm particularly sensitive to *Amazon Speak* because I write it daily on behalf of my clients.

The other reason I'm suspicious of ALL CAPS!!! is that there are groups on Facebook whose members have advocated this trick – caps and all – as a good way to get a competitor in trouble. These nasty players are the Ferengi[4] of the Amazon seller world. They see the world as "us" and "them." The idea of "co-opetition" or "friendly competitor" is anathema to them. It is kill or be killed in their world. I'm not exaggerating. I've read their posts. I've been at the receiving end of their unethical practices.

Some people will read this chapter and learn something useful from it. Some will read it as a handbook to take down their competitors, and others will burn me in effigy for telling their secrets. Luckily the latter two are the minority (just like the Ferengi).

SOLUTION: The best way to combat this trick is to really pay attention to your negative seller feedback and customer messages. Many of my clients are large sellers. They have customer service teams and are somewhat removed from the day-to-day complaints of their customers. A lot of all-FBA sellers don't get many customer emails – just seller feedback. Amazon handles most complaints for them. After we get our clients reinstated, many of them now run these reports at least weekly, so they can see

---

4 The **Ferengi** are a fictional extraterrestrial race from the *Star Trek* universe. They and their culture are characterized by a mercantile obsession with profit and trade, and their constant efforts to swindle unwary customers into unfair deals. https://en.wikipedia.org/wiki/Ferengi

what is going on. They have also trained their customer service team to know which complaints they need to act on right away.

Acting quickly takes a lot of wind out of these evil sellers' sails. Amazon warns and suspends sellers who are not paying attention. They reward and reinstate those who do. If you contact the complainer through Amazon's platform (which I always recommend), there is a record of your responsiveness and willingness to address the issue.

YOU NEED TO KNOW: Sometimes the evil sellers are dumb enough to actually make the claims themselves, which makes it pretty easy to spot and stop them. Smarter ones ask like-minded friends and relatives to order the products and complain, which makes it harder to uncover the evil-doer unless they do it over and over again. This is why I started collecting names – I started to recognize people.

There was one seller who sent the product to her mother as a gift, but made the complaint herself. I recognized her from a Facebook group. I guess she forgot that we can see the orders or maybe thought she wouldn't be recognized. She's not playing this game anymore.

TRICK: *Policy Violations.* In the previous trick, you know the name of your accuser. You don't know if they are a real customer or not. In this one, you don't know anything. Your competitor has filed a policy violation against you, which means you'll never see who sent it. Amazon sends you a vague message about "customer complaints," but you can't find a single claim anywhere that helps you figure out what happened with that ASIN. This lack of evidence is often the only evidence you have that the claim was filed by a competitor.

I see this especially when my client is listing on someone else's private label product (wrongly or rightly – a lot of those "private label" products are generics bought in China with no distinguishing features). The other seller buys the item and then claims to Amazon that it is fake or missing parts or unauthentic because it doesn't have whatever whoop-de-doo they've added to the product. The guy with the reflexology chart, for example, was sending his customers a PDF of a foot chart when they bought the product (a clever use of Feedback Genius). In the warehouse, his product and my client's product were *exactly* the same. Nonetheless, Amazon sided with the competitor.

In this case my client was in the wrong, and I had to tell him so. Our plan reflected his contrition and learning from the experience. In another case, a competitor was selling a generic product but had added his company name to the listing as the manufacturer (his company had created the listing in the first place). While this is utterly wrong, Amazon sided with the competitor. This was not a private label product. The competitor had added nothing to the product. My client rightly listed his product on that listing. Nonetheless, he lost. After he was reinstated, he created a new listing and sold his product there. Then his competitor listed under my client's listing and filed a policy violation again! It was outrageous.

Despite proving the legitimacy of my client's product – twice – against the same competitor complainer, my client was suspended again! This is Joly Stick's story from the beginning of the book. It took months, but Joly ultimately fixed the problem by confronting the competitor directly at his office. We escalated the problem high inside Amazon (we targeted our man at an industry event) to get a permanent note put on Joly's account, so he wouldn't be suspended again by a competitor on these particular products.

It is unreal that we had to go up to Jeff Bezos' inner circle to get the help we needed. It shouldn't be that hard to get someone to really listen to your case. It was a five-minute conversation. Most sellers don't have the financial resources to pursue a case like this (the conference registration fee was very expensive, plus flight and hotel). Most people don't have Joly's incredible drive and determination. He was suspended a total of four times over six months. He didn't just track down his competitor; he tracked down the actual person who was filing these claims.

In Joly's case, he knew who had made the complaint. There was only one other competitor it could be. Both were fierce about this product because it was worth more than $1 million in sales each year. It is one of those unassuming and boring products – like the paper clip – that apparently no one can live without.

Electronics is like that. This category has more evil sellers than almost any other category. When a client tells me they sell in electronics, I immediately wonder if there's an evil seller at work. There are also a lot of shifty, shady selling practices going on in electronics, like inventory that fell off of trucks, for example. For the record, I'll state that bad business practices make you extremely vulnerable to being suspended, whether an evil seller is at work or not. If you can't tell me exactly where your inventory came from, we won't lie for you. However, I can work with the truth, no matter how awful.

Of course evil is not confined to certain categories. In a case involving party supplies (seriously?!), the competitor claimed my client was selling an incomplete and faulty product. He opened the package when he got it, removed some items, took a picture of it, and made his claim with Amazon. My client had a contact inside Amazon who sent him the complaint and picture. This peek inside of a seller's account is really rare (and not authorized by Amazon) and gave us a lot of insight into the whole process.

My client was suspended for something he didn't do. We also know this is the case because he had Amazon check ALL of his units in the FBA warehouse. All of them were sealed and complete. It was spite, pure and simple. It took weeks to get him reinstated. When he was, the competitor had the nerve to contact him through Amazon's platform and try to get him to raise his prices to where they could "all make more money." When my client noted that he was not the lowest-priced seller on the listing, the other seller pointed out that the overall price had been higher the few weeks while he had been gone. What a piece of work.

By the way, it is forbidden to price-fix. This guy was crazy. We don't know who he is (he went through Amazon's platform), but Amazon does. I doubt he'll contact my client ever again. We filed our own policy violation. We had to. If that evidence of price fixing had not been firmly addressed, the evil seller could have accused *my client* of price fixing in a subsequent policy violation.

Another form of this trick is often played by manufacturers. Surprised? There are a lot of manufacturers who don't want their products sold on Amazon.com. Online prices undercut their pricing and exclusivity agreements with their retail partners. Or it may be that they want all online sales to come through them. Regardless, they will try a number of tactics to scare a third-party seller off their listing. It is fast and easy for them to get what they want by filing bogus policy violations.

Amazon doesn't always support a manufacturer's position on pricing (she says dryly). Amazon itself breaks manufacturers' minimum advertised price (MAP) rules all the time. But they do pay attention to policy violations, which is why manufacturers use them.

Regardless of the fact that it is a manufacturer filing the violation, it is always up to you to prove that your product is authentic and/or legal for you to sell. If you are buying your merchandise from retail stores, dealers or liquidators, you are out of luck. The manufacturer will refuse to acknowledge the legitimacy of any source except the manufacturer itself, and sometimes an authorized reseller/distributor. Amazon will accept retail arbitrage *if* the UPC code is printed on the receipt with the name of the product. You won't find acceptable receipts at a dollar store or thrift store. The same problem applies at many discount stores, such as TJ Maxx or Marshalls. You can't prove you bought legitimate merchandise, which is a serious offense in Amazon's eyes. Recall, also, that Amazon considers products bought from retail arbitrage to be Used so you may have additional issues with "Used sold as New" to deal with now.

Manufacturers and other rights-holders are the ones who file most copyright infringement claims. Amazon takes these seriously when brought to them by an attorney. At that point, they will suspend you (and everyone else) from that listing and insist you resolve the issue with the rights-holder. Sometimes they will also suspend you from selling altogether. Determining the legitimacy of the claim is not Amazon's job. They stay out of it. My observation is that some rights-holders with legitimate claims (you are using their picture in your listing, for example) will work with you. They just want the problem fixed. Others who never return your emails and calls? Suspicious. In this case, though, there is not much you can do besides stop selling the product.

While you know who your accuser is in this case, I mention it here as a very serious policy violation. I have a client who has been banned from selling because of one copyright infringement claim we cannot resolve because the so-called rights-holder won't call my client back. Even though my client has deleted the ASIN from his inventory, it is not enough in this case.

SOLUTION: If you are suspicious of bad seller or manufacturer behavior, try to track down the order – usually, they've ordered your product. You might be able to narrow it down your possible accusers that way. The best protection is to have legitimate invoices or to buy your product from stores that provide complete receipts.

In terms of copyright infringement, try your best to resolve the issue. If the complaint is legit, the rights-holder will usually at least answer you and tell you what you need to do in order to sell again. Once they are satisfied, they will tell Amazon (they have their own email address with Amazon) that you are OK and you'll be allowed to sell again. If it is a ploy, you'll never win. You won't be able to sell the product on Amazon.

YOU NEED TO KNOW: The happy Amazon workers who read your appeals are not necessarily business-savvy. What seems obvious to you is not going to be obvious to them. They try to see all sellers as equal and don't take sides in disputes. Trying to explain how a competitor is deliberately screwing you is a difficult task, which is why we try to avoid it. Joly Stick had to track down one of the top guys at Amazon to make his case. Even the helpful trade show booth workers (so young! so enthusiastic!) couldn't understand it very well.

We try very hard to reinstate our clients first and then help them address the competitor situation. It is better to make your case from a position of strength. It sounds less like an excuse for failure and more like a real problem.

TRICK: *Package not Received/Damaged in Shipping/Late Delivery.* This trick is used by buyers as a way to get free product and by sellers as a way to hurt an MF competitor. If you are MF, you are particularly vulnerable to getting suspended for performance issues. Most MF sellers use USPS, which makes them even more vulnerable. There may be tracking, but the letter carrier is not always diligent in using it. This means a package might show it is "in transit" long after it has been delivered. It is often nearly impossible to track down a lost package or figure out where it got lost. I've seen emails where the seller is telling the customer to go to their local post office and see if the package is there. Are you kidding?!? That is begging for negative feedback.

Moreover, most packages aren't insured, so the seller is losing money when a product does not reach its destination or is damaged. USPS is notorious for losing or delaying packages, which leads to lots of unhappy customers, which then leads to you getting suspended for one or all of the reasons listed above.

I've seen clients send out replacement products three times and still the buyer mysteriously never received it. This problem seems especially acute in the UK with the Royal Mail. One client was particularly frustrated by a buyer who kept swearing he never received the package, even after my client had personally contacted the mail carrier who swore he had delivered it personally.

This guy was obviously a scammer. I couldn't tell if he was a seller. After the third failed delivery my client asked, "What do I say to this guy?" She didn't use my answer which was: "Dear X, I'm sorry that your penis is still so small. We are doing our best to rectify the situation." Yep. He was scamming her on a male enhancement product. We giggled thinking about him resorting to stealing to get his fix. There are some things you just can't make up. Truth is stranger than fiction. Ultimately, she refunded him and refused to send out again.

That, by the way, is the best solution if you suspect the buyer is lying about a lost package. Refund them instantly, apologize and don't send out any more units. Refunding generally closes a case with Amazon. The buyer can't file an A-to-Z claim. I have some clients that refund after the first time something is lost and refuse to send out again.

I've had several UK clients tell me, "No one pays extra for tracking with the Royal Mail." Except Amazon. They pay for tracking, and they expect their sellers to do the same. It is not a requirement in the UK right now, but they punish you heavily for all the side-effects of not tracking – lost product, late delivery, frequent refunds and repeat shipments. The UK is small. Many items are routinely delivered in a day or two at the most, so express mail is rarely used. Tracking isn't as common. But this is about fraud reduction and getting support from Amazon if something does go awry. If you have tracking and can show that the product was delivered on time, they won't hold it against you if the customer can't find it or is a fraudster.

MF seller accounts are often riddled with performance complaints for lost and damaged products, and there is nothing they can do about it except 1) upgrade their carrier and 2) buy business insurance that covers their losses from shipping. This is expensive for most sellers and only makes sense if they are shipping at a certain level.

One thing I can say definitively for all sellers who are fulfilling UK or European orders from the U.S.: "You are a suspension waiting to happen." I've seen the craziest things, like shipping nail polish to England from California or thumb drives to Germany from New York. To make it even remotely feasible financially, my clients are working with cheapo carriers that provide no accountability or guarantee of delivery or timeliness. If there is tracking, it ends at the destination country's borders. Their packages often get held up at customs, which angers the buyers no end as they have to go and collect their package and pay a storage fee for the privilege.

SOLUTION: No one likes this one, but switching to 100% FBA fixes most performance issues and makes you less vulnerable to these claims. My nail polish client complained that there was no margin if he had to go with a more reliable carrier like DHL. I said to him, "you need to sell better merchandise than nail polish." If your margins are that small, you are selling the wrong product. Because he didn't want to consider a better carrier, I asked him to consider FBA. Nail polish is small and lightweight. He could send a lot of product to Amazon's UK warehouse for a small price per unit and fix all his fulfillment issues overnight.

I'm surprised how many MF sellers don't understand FBA. They think it is expensive, but I'm able to show them how they can continue to make the same money – and sometimes better – by switching to FBA. The trick, of course, is charging more than MF. Many of my clients are skeptical that they can charge more money for their inventory. They are used to competing against other MF sellers on price only. Once they see how many people are willing to pay more for free two-day shipping, they are usually pretty enthusiastic.

I know I'm biased here because I've been selling FBA from the first day I started selling, but my life is a lot easier than most of my clients lives. I run a consulting practice, write books, speak and...oh yeah...sell on Amazon.com. I couldn't do that without FBA. I'd be spending all my time shipping out small packages, dealing with customer complaints, or running a warehouse. I'd rather prepare reinstatement plans.

The other solution I suggest is turning on the setting that allows Amazon to automatically take care of your returns/refunds. FBA sellers get this automatically, and MF sellers can too. You tell Amazon your parameters, and they make it as simple as one click for customers to arrange to return their unwanted product, get a replacement or a refund. The system generates a pre-paid return shipping label that customers print off at home.

By making it easy for your customers to return their products or get a refund, you reduce the number of unhappy customers significantly. This won't stop an evil seller or fraudulent buyer from complaining, of course, but it does reduce the overall total number of imperfect orders you have, which makes you more able to withstand an attack. You have enough on your plate. Let Amazon take over the bulk of your customer service.

<u>YOU NEED TO KNOW:</u> All customer inquiries count against you. It is considered an "imperfect order" if the customer needs to contact you for any reason. The more difficult you make it to get a refund/replacement, the more likely you are to have multiple complaints for the same order. Each one counts against you: A-to-Z claims, returns, a customer email and a refund. A competitor can attack you very subtly, hoping to rack up many points against you over and over again.

TRICK: ***Multiple Returns on the Same Day/Multiple Negative Feedbacks on the Same Day.*** This dirty trick uses Amazon's velocity triggers against you. If Amazon sees multiple returns, inquiries and/or negative feedbacks for an ASIN on the same day, it goes into shut-down mode. *Danger, Will Robinson!*5 The robots freak out. At best they'll suspend you on the listing. At worst, they'll suspend your account.

Velocity is easy to manipulate. An evil seller buys multiple units of your product. Then they decide to return it all on the same day for "defective" or "inauthentic" or "Not as Described." Amazon's robots don't see this as one order of three units, for example. They see this as three separate orders being returned. Boom! That's three defective claims on one product in one day.

A similar trick is for multiple people (friends of the evil seller) to buy the same product and then all file negative feedback at the same time. These are actually pretty easy to detect because their feedback is almost identical. Obviously they've discussed it beforehand, so the feedback is not natural. The words are the same. They often use *Amazon Speak*. This also triggers the robots. One seller saw the same typo on several negative feedbacks for the same product so he knew they were co-ordinated, cut-and-paste comments. He successfully defended himself against their attack and got their feedback permanently removed (not just a strike-through).

<u>SOLUTION:</u> There's not much you can do in terms of prevention except keep your stats high. You want your negative feedback rate to be less than 3%, your ODR to be less than 1% and your returns under 3%. That way a blitz attack won't hurt you as much. Most of my clients had worse stats when they were blitzed, so it pushed them into suspension.

---

5 Catchphrase from the 1960's American television series "Lost in Space" as spoken by The Robot character.

YOU NEED TO KNOW: Amazon does not hold negative seller feedback against you immediately. Your ODR stats are based on 90 days of sales. If you can get a feedback removed within a week or so of it happening, it is like it never happened. I've dropped below 90% positive feedback several times in my selling career, when I got several negative feedbacks in a row. I was able to get them removed quickly and bounced right back up. I'm currently at 100%, and so are most of my clients after we are done working together.

It is much easier to get negative feedback removed when you are not suspended. You can use the automated system, which puts the robots to work for you instead of against you. Many feedback removal requests are handled automatically. Others are sent to Seller Central for someone to review. One of the worst problems you can get is A-to-Z claims *that Amazon resolves.* Each one is -500 points on your stats. If you jump in and resolve the situation with a refund/return before Amazon closes the case, it won't count against you. The record is still there, but it notes that the seller resolved the case. When you look at their summary A-to-Z claims report, it only counts the ones Amazon closed. I've not seen a lot of evil sellers use A-to-Z claims to bring down a competitor – probably because Amazon is so closely involved in the situation. However, clients with lots of A-to-Z claims are highly vulnerable to attack on their metrics.

TRICK: *False Claims in Returns Report.* This is not usually a standalone strategy. The evil seller will choose a false reason for the return to ding your metrics for returns and possibly "Not as Described" or "Defective." Because a lot of weasely buyers use the same technique to get out of paying shipping for the return, it is very hard to tell if this is a competitor or a dishonest buyer. However, we see this used a lot with the velocity strategy, previously discussed. It's a trifecta – multiple returns, negative feedback and a policy violation listed as the reasons for the return. Normally a dishonest buyer won't necessarily ding you for negative feedback or send back multiple units. Frequently the customer just changed their mind and doesn't want to have to pay to ship the item back. If you see the trifecta at work, consider that an evil seller may be after you.

SOLUTION: This is one of the most infuriating of Amazon's policies. It is unfair to sellers and punishes us for the dishonesty of others. A school of thought says Amazon should allow us to offer free return shipping to everyone. No more buyers "forced" to lie to get what they really want – a consequence-free return for a product they no longer want for whatever reason. Obviously, this could be really expensive and horribly abused. The sellers only like the idea because they would no longer be punished for a buyer's bad behavior.

In terms of what you can do? Not much. In Plans that I've written for clients, we've tracked consistent reasons customers have stated in their emails to my clients and in negative feedback. When we find the returns that are troubling to Amazon, we dissect them. On some of them, it is pretty easy to tell the customer is lying or to see the trifecta play.

Keeping a regular eye on your returns report helps. You can see patterns. If you see a particular ASIN getting a lot of returns, you need to suspend that listing and check into it. There might be something actually wrong with the product. If there is an uptick in "Not as Described" or "defective" claims across multiple ASINs, it might be a seller attack. Forewarned is forearmed.

YOU NEED TO KNOW: It is against Amazon policy for a buyer to blackmail a seller ("I'll file an A-to-Z Claim if you don't give me a full refund without my returning the product!"), and you should report that buyer. While I don't know what Amazon does to the buyer, you should report every time it happens to you – even if you refund the blackmailer. This holds true for lying to get free shipping, too. Amazon may not do anything about it, but they note it. Buyers have a lifetime number of free returns. Last I heard it was 25. Once they reach that number, they are forbidden to do it ever again.

Amazon knows and keeps track of people who abuse their policies, and they don't let them get away with it forever. If you can prove that the buyer only changed their tune to get free shipping, Amazon will notate that buyer's account. Proof can be in the form of an email from the buyer telling you one thing ("I changed my mind") and then claiming another. Guess who knows best how to manipulate the system? Third-party sellers. They are usually the ones threatening you and usually the ones who suddenly have a defective product they want to return. Not always, of course, but you have to consider there are *millions* of third-party sellers out there. They buy stuff on Amazon, too.

TRICK: *Tie up Inventory.* I've only seen this a couple of times. A competitor will buy multiple units – maybe all – of your inventory for a discontinued, rare or hard-to-get item. Near the end of your return period, they will return some or all of the units with a bogus complaint. You get the velocity problem, and the policy violation, *and* you lost the use of your inventory for a month or so – possibly longer if Amazon determines that the units are unsellable. (I'm assuming you sell FBA here – obviously if you are MF, the units are sent to you for inspection.)

What was your competitor doing with the inventory during that time? They were probably selling it on your Amazon listing and possibly on eBay. They might even have had Amazon fulfill their eBay orders for them. Whatever they couldn't sell in a month came back to you. They made money off of what they sold and got their money back on the rest.

While this is despicable behavior, there is little you can do about it. As long as they don't abuse Prime when they do it, you can't catch them out. Because most orders like this are over $35 and people are getting free shipping anyway, they don't care about getting it in two days. While this is explicitly against Amazon policy, sellers flip things on Amazon all the time. It is called "Amazon Arbitrage." The difference is that most people who find inventory this way don't return it and lie about its condition. They keep it and sell it even if it takes longer than 30 days. I have yet to see Amazon suspend someone for practicing Amazon Arbitrage.

SOLUTION: Be skeptical of large orders that take most or all of your inventory of a particular ASIN. If the buyer comes back to you 30 days later with complaints, dispute their claims with Amazon. The velocity hit could be crippling. You have to allow them to return the merchandise if the request is within 30 days. But you don't have to take it lying down. Provide invoices or whatever you need to show your product was new when it went to them. Tell Amazon that you suspect bad competitor behavior and are worried Amazon will count each item as a separate return for that ASIN. Tell them you want it to be noted on your record. Ask them to check and see if the buyer is a third-party seller or closely linked to a third-party seller. Thank them for their help and keep a record of their response. This will help if you are suspended for this complaint at a later date.

YOU NEED TO KNOW: I hate to mention this, but you need to know that bringing up these issues with Amazon (the multiple returns, the bogus "defective" or "inauthentic") could trigger the suspension immediately. Or you might trigger an account review. Or you might get an auto-generated letter that says they want you to create a Plan of Action to deal with these issues. It adds insult to injury and a real kick in the teeth to sellers who try hard to do the right thing. This is because the robots are running Seller Performance. It is not personal. I still believe you are better off taking a proactive stance.

Amazon tends to reward sellers who are responsive and proactive. Grit your teeth and point out to them that YOU brought the issue to them ("see case #123456") and that YOU are concerned because YOU suspect malicious intention on behalf of the buyer. Ask them if they can check and see if he is a third-party seller on Amazon's platform or related to one. They won't tell you what they find, but if you are right, that seller will be getting a warning about manipulating the platform among other things.

Oh, and write the darn Plan. Nobody gets reinstated without the Plan even when they are the victim, even when there really is no Plan to write that makes sense: "I plan to avoid evil competitors in the future by wearing garlic and sprinkling holy water on my merchandise." In all seriousness, these are tough Plans to write. I worry about them more because it is hard to show that my client has learned something and made meaningful changes to make sure it doesn't happen again. After all, they never did anything wrong in the first place.

REINSTATEMENT NOTES:

1. Malicious sellers are real, and they are organized. They swap tips in Facebook groups and on other social sites. You are not immune.
2. Amazon will tell you about ASIN changes but not picture changes.
3. If you are regularly checking your returns, imperfect orders, customer messages and negative feedback reports, you will see possible problems more quickly.
4. These reports will help you identify the claims if you are ever suspended.
5. If your metrics are strong, you are better able to withstand an attack.
6. Remember, the robots can't actually read. Nuances like "not fake" are lost on them. They only see keyword triggers like "fake."
7. To help you fend off attacks, you need to close these vulnerabilities:
   - No liquidators.
   - No eBay dealers.
   - No drop shippers.

- No retail arbitrage in stores with poor receipts that don't include the UPC code.
- No buying from a guy who knows a guy. If you can't back up the authenticity of your inventory, you're cooked.

8. If you MF, you are highly vulnerable to performance claims by evil competitors.

9. If you see *Amazon Speak* in an email or negative feedback, be suspicious. Only insiders and other sellers use it.

10. The easier you make it for buyers to return their merchandise, the less likely they are to lie or complain about it.

11. Look for the double- or triple-whammy of false claims, negative feedback and bogus return reasons – these combined often signify a third-party seller who knows exactly what they are doing to your account.

12. Don't let the bad guys win. When it is appropriate, fight back. Report them.

13. Be proactive in protecting your account. Watch your performance notifications closely.

Part II

Suspension Prevention

6

Reclaim Your Account

" **I** haven't slept in days." "I just fired two more employees today." "I'm declaring bankruptcy on Monday." "I don't know how to tell my employees what happened." How many times have I heard heartbreaking stories like that in the past few months? How many texts and calls have I gotten after midnight? How many people have cried on the phone with me? The answer is "way too many." Amazon's decisions don't just affect sellers. They affect entire communities and families.

There is a heightened anxiety among the Amazon seller community right now. People are getting suspended every day. Those who haven't been suspended wonder if they're next. Sellers feel helpless. Even those who have been successfully reinstated are anxious. Their confidence in themselves to manage their accounts and to solve business problems has been shaken. They've been faced with a cold, heartless, irrational beast that they used to think was a friendly partner. *Traumatized* comes close to describing it, but that word isn't big enough.

Mrs. Sowerberry couldn't understand it. She had submitted invoice after invoice to Amazon – exactly as they asked – and still they denied her appeal! It slowly dawned on her. She was banned! They weren't going to read any more appeals from her. After 10 years and $10M a year worth of sales it couldn't just be over, could it? And she did everything they asked … didn't she? She was dizzy and exhausted from thinking in circles.

As of this writing, there are five sellers I was not able to reinstate. Three of them really upset me. Two were longshots from the beginning and knew it, but the other three didn't deserve what happened to them. Their "crimes" weren't any more heinous than anyone else's. They failed because there is no one behind the curtain looking deeply and carefully into each situation. I'm not dissing the workers at Amazon. They have their orders, their processes and their marching orders. They are not rewarded for creative thinking, and they are not authorized to make exceptions. I am angry at the soulless system.

Amazon loves its customers but seems to forget that its sellers are customers and people too – people who usually work pretty damn hard and make Amazon a lot of money. One of my unsuccessful reinstatements was a small retail arbitrage seller who had the wrong receipt. It didn't have the UPC code on it. Nothing we said changed Amazon's position. Even with a picture of the price tag (with the store's internal product number) compared to the receipt was not good enough. It was so unjust that I still feel bitter. My client was not a counterfeit seller. She was buying from retail stores, for Pete's sake!

It is too late for her and the other four, but it is not too late for you.

Knowledge is power. Awareness is warning. Action is prevention.

This section is about you taking it back – your account, your business, your sleep, your health, your life. If you are suspended, I hope what you learn here helps you get reinstated. If you are not suspended, I hope this section empowers you. For all of you wondering if another suspension will drop on your head like an anvil, there are steps you can take to protect yourself.

For some of you, this will be a tough section. You will reject what I'm saying. It is hard to realize and admit that your own business processes may be putting you at risk. You don't want to hear that practices that were fine in your previous life and on other platforms don't work here. I understand that. That is why Amazon suspends. Suspension is a crude instrument that batters the innocent alongside the guilty, but it certainly makes a seller compliant and open to hearing new things. My hope for you is that you don't need to be suspended to learn new things.

Some of these actions may or may not apply to your situation. With so much seller variation on the platform it is challenging to be universal in my advice:

STEP ONE: *TAKE RESPONSIBILITY*

Amazon is not interested in excuses – no matter how valid – or claims that someone is out to get you. What they want to know is that you take responsibility and will fix the problem. Most of our Plans get approved, I believe, because my clients state exactly what they did and what happened. They tell about the mistakes they made. They learn from their experiences.

Remember when I said earlier that I can deal with almost anything as long as it is the truth? I have gotten clients reinstated who were selling counterfeit; who bought from illegal sources; who had the worst customer service I have ever, ever seen; who tried to trump up invoices; who sold expired, used, stale, dirty and broken items again and again and again. They cheated their customers. They sold in foreign markets with no idea of what they were doing.

When they understood how Amazon saw them, and when they understood how their customers were affected, they felt badly. They took responsibility, and they cleaned up their act. One of my colleagues once said to me, "Do you think any of these guys actually implement their plans, or is it just lip service to get reinstated?" I told him, "They know that if they don't, they'll be suspended again." And most of them do implement their plans. How do I know this? Because we help them do it. I talk more about that in section three.

My point here is that my clients not only take responsibility for what happened, they fix the problem. That is true responsibility, not lip service. If Amazon sends you a policy warning, or if your performance metrics take a dive, jump on it. Fix it. Tell Amazon what you are doing. It will go a long way in your favor if you are suspended and might even keep you from being suspended.

When you look at your own account and feel helpless, remember that you are not. You are responsible. You can find the trouble spots and fix them. You can improve your metrics and your customers' experiences. You can be the partner that Amazon wants, but first you have to accept that it is your responsibility to do so.

STEP TWO: *BE HUMBLE AND TEACHABLE - IT PROBABLY IS YOUR FAULT*

As a group, my clients are extraordinary business people. While they may be captains of industry (in some cases), they are also practical people. They may not like what I have to say, but they listen. They recognize that they've made mistakes before, so they may be wrong in this situation, too.

Often they will say to us, "Tell me what I need to do and I'll do it." I really wish that Jeff Bezos and the other customer maniacs at Amazon could see how fabulous their sellers are. Not perfect, but fabulous all the same. They work their asses off to get reinstated, not only for the money that is being held hostage, but because they worry about their employees. Every client-employer I've worked with paid his/her employees while suspended for as long as they could. Some took cash out of their personal accounts to keep their employees going.

When you get a warning from or if you get suspended by Amazon, you will probably be mad. This is natural. After your emotions calm a little bit, try to see what Amazon is attempting to do with the suspension. Is there a process that could be improved? Is there something more you could be doing for your customers? Is it time to move some inventory to FBA? Be teachable. It probably is your fault. With only a few exceptions, my clients had made mistakes that contributed to their suspension.

It wasn't as out of the blue as they thought. They just didn't see the signs. You are in a better position than they were before they got suspended. You can find the signs and make the changes now.

STEP THREE: *READ YOUR AMAZON REPORTS*

Amazon provides a bewildering number of reports to its sellers, and it hides the most important ones. Go figure. It would be so helpful if they would provide a report showing you how many hard and soft hits you have on your account at any given moment but they don't. We have to find them ourselves. When we have a new client, the first thing we do is an assessment. This gives us insight into what is actually happening with the account.

The first three reports we pull are the Imperfect Orders report, the Negative Feedback report and the Returns report. We also read all their customer inquiries for as far back as it takes for us to understand what our client's customers are saying to Amazon about our client.

Imperfect Orders is what Amazon calls any order where a customer contacts you or Amazon for any reason. This can be as simple as an email inquiry or as serious as an A-to-Z claim. Returns and negative feedback are also included. On a spreadsheet, you can quickly see what kind of problem you have the most. (It is usually returns but not always.) If you are having a lot of problems with a particular ASIN, we can see it here. The Imperfect Orders report is our starting point – the compass pointing in the right direction.

Negative Feedback is where a lot of your customer complaints are coming from, of course. Someone says you are selling Used as New? It is probably in this report. Once you find the complaint, you can delve into the situation and find out what happened. Is it damage in shipping? Poor packaging? This is where you begin. If you are one of those sellers who quickly gets negative feedback removed, you will need to view your deleted feedback as well as current. It is possible the robots are triggering off a keyword in a removed feedback.

If you scroll through your negative feedback on your screen in Seller Central, you will also see the removed feedback. If you use Feedback Genius, you can see your removed and current negative feedback on one report.

Returns has two locations in your Seller Central, depending on whether you sell MF or FBA. You'll find it under fulfillment reports (FBA) and orders (MF). If you are both, you will have both. For some reason, Amazon gives its MF sellers a lot more to work with. The FBA report shows you the reason the customer chose for the return, but not their complaint. The MF report will often have quotes and details like the negative feedback report. It makes sense if you think about it because if Amazon is handling your returns, they aren't going to ding you for FBA issues like damage in shipping, so the specific customer complaint is irrelevant. They WILL ding the MF guys, of course.

This report can be a rich source of information about problem ASINs. If you see someone returning multiples of one ASIN in a day, you know to suspect evil seller activity on that ASIN. If you see a lot of returns for an ASIN in general, you need to find out what is going on. Giving Amazon invoices for your inventory isn't enough if your customers all legitimately suspect an item is fake. Think about the situation previously cited. Is there something going on here that you should fix?

What I'll usually see in an FBA returns report is a lot of Defective, Damaged in Shipping and Not as Described. Once again, I'm looking to see if there are any ASINs that are causing a disproportionate percentage of the returns. Yes, some of the buyers are lying to get free return shipping. You have to let that go if you can. It will only aggravate you. If it is clear they are lying (they told you one thing and Amazon another), then report them and move on.

A-to-Z Claims reports are only available to MF sellers. If you are FBA, your customers are not allowed to file A-to-Z claims. Amazon takes care of them. I've seen accounts with dozens to nearly 100 A-to-Z claims in 90 days. Let me tell you now, that report should have zero claims that Amazon had to address. Not zero A-to-Z claims – those are part of business – but zero where they had to refund and close the claim.

When one of these claims is filed, Amazon is *not* your mediator. They are your punisher. You can and should tell them what happened if there is a side to the story that is missing. However, you need to take care of the customer first and *fast*. If Amazon closes the case, it counts against you. If you refund the customer first, they don't count the A-to-Z claim against you.

Because I've seen a lot of misinformation about this online, let me repeat again: it all stays on your record as happening, but ONLY the cases Amazon closes and refunds are counted against you. Since each Amazon-closed claim is -500 to your metrics, this is an important point. Unlike negative feedback, you can't come back and fix it later.

Messages are not a report, but they are real-time information for you. This is where your customers contact you through the platform asking questions, wanting refunds, complaining and so on. We have seen both appalling and awesome customer service. The companies who do it best have polite, thoughtful form letters that they use over and over again. At worst, we see sellers arguing with their customers, accusing them of lying (and worse), paying only measly partial refunds when it is their (the sellers') fault and much more.

STEP FOUR: *KEEP TRACK OF YOUR METRICS*

In addition to keeping track of customer complaints, you need to keep a close, close eye on your performance metrics. This is more relevant to MF sellers than FBA, but even FBA sellers are vulnerable to faulty products and negative feedback.

Amazon's rules about late shipments have changed in the past year, for example. It used to be that a shipment counted as shipped when you uploaded the tracking code. Now it doesn't count until the carrier picks up and scans the package. That is a huge difference that immediately turned good sellers into poor sellers overnight. Many sellers would upload tracking at the end of the day, and have pick up the next. Now their inventory is considered late if they do that. I tell them to make UPS come in the evening or to deliver their packages themselves to the late-night drop-off if they have to.

A client of mine on the East Coast who used a drop shipper to send out his orders often didn't upload shipping data until the next morning because of the time difference. He had to change that behavior and now takes care of it every night so he's not considered late by Amazon. His packages were leaving on time and reaching the customers on time, but they weren't getting recorded on time.

Some clients got in trouble because they were confirming their orders before they were actually picked up by the carrier. This is a no-no. You will get warned and then worse. Don't confirm your orders until after they are picked up. Amazon is not fooled, and they are not amused.

Late shipments are just the beginning of course. There are late deliveries – a problem that hurts a lot of my clients who fulfill overseas orders from the U.S. – lost packages, damage in shipping, faulty product, poor packaging, late customer inquiry response and more. These metrics are captured on your summary pages but may not tell the whole story. You should look at the actual data to see if there are patterns and problems you can proactively fix.

If you have a problem that repeats, you need to fix it. It seems obvious, but I'm often surprised at how long my clients sold obviously faulty product, continued to sell even though their chosen carrier wasn't delivering their products on time, were told there were repackages and used products in their inventory (sold as New) but didn't inspect them themselves. The list goes on and on. If your customers or Amazon metrics are telling you something, you need to act.

For my clients who have trouble responding to their customers fast enough, for example, I have them download the Amazon Seller App to their phone. It will notify you instantly if there is a customer message, so you can respond immediately. I have my clients commit to responding to their emails at least twice a day during the week and once a day on weekends and holidays.

Lastly, be sure you are tracking your *real* metrics. Now that you know there are only five "hard hits" a year allowed to your account, it means that every counterfeit claim is important and you can't let them go unanswered. Because we don't know what the other "hard hits" are, we tell our clients to assume that they are all hard hits. If there is a policy violation, it needs to be addressed. Period. You can't afford to let anything build up.

When you address a policy violation with Amazon, be sure to ask them to put an internal annotation on your account that the ASIN was not counterfeit (or whatever the claim is). This will help if you are ever suspended in the future for that ASIN.

STEP FIVE: *FIX YOUR LISTINGS*

This has got to be one of the most confusing areas of Amazon policy and violations. On the one hand, we are told that everyone should list under one listing. There shouldn't be multiples. THEN we are told that if there is the slightest variation whatsoever with the product, it needs a separate listing. This is where things get all fuzzy because there may not really be any variation. All those private label guys who think they are so smart slapping a label on a generic product are creating confusion on the platform for everyone – buyers and sellers.

If you are going to private label, do it right and create a truly different value-add product. (Whoops! Where did that soapbox come from?). Back to listings. I've seen sellers who genuinely try to do the right thing and clean up their listings and still get into trouble. Here are a few pointers:

- *Don't list your generic under a branded listing.* Yes, I know. It's the same product, but Amazon doesn't see it that way. If the listing creator is registered, they can kick you off the listing at best or get you suspended at worst. Make a new listing.

- *Don't sell generic products as private label.* Equally problematic. It causes confusion and can get you shut down. Make a real value-added change to the product that you can defend. Your picture and description should clearly tell buyers what is different about your product from other, similar products.
- *Don't deliver your product by email.* The guy who emailed a foot reflexology chart to his customers as part of his private label offering was clever, BUT what he did is against Amazon policy. Why? Because not everyone will open and read their email. Many people don't even give Amazon their real email address. That chart needed to be a part of every single package that was delivered, technically. He was sending out a product with missing parts. When Amazon finds out, they will shut his listing down (at best) with a warning. It is OK to offer the chart as a customer-friendly afterthought, but if it is part of the listing, it needs to be in the box. I send recipes to buyers of one of my holiday bundles. It is a nice-to-have, not part of the product offering.
- *Register your brand.* If you own it, register it. It will save you hassle down the road and allow you to defend your listing. It also blocks other sellers from making changes to your ASIN. They can still sell on it, technically, but they can't mess with it.
- *Look for copyright infringement.* This applies mostly to listings you create. Did you take the picture off the internet? You could be vulnerable. Is the brand not properly listed with ® or ™? You could be vulnerable. Did you lift your product description from the manufacturer's website? You could be vulnerable. Not all brands vigorously defend their trademarks online, but those that do...watch out! Make sure you take your own pictures (that meet Amazon's exacting standards!), write your own descriptions and use the correct symbols.
- *Don't use condition notes for variations.* I see this often. Your condition notes are exclusively to describe the condition of the packaging or the product, *not* for variations. New is New. There should be nothing else to say. No marketing copy, no claims of fast shipping. Nothing. New is New. For used products, like a CD, you might say "Used-Good: Scuffed cover with scratches and cracked case. CD is in playable condition with very minor scratches." This is a physical description of the product but the implication is that it is *in no way*

different from the New product otherwise. You would NOT say "CD is missing liner notes and promotional poster." Used products must be complete. You would NOT say "This is the 1978 version" when the listing is the latest version *unless* that is a variation that is noted in the ***description***. You usually only see this with books, and this book isn't long enough for me to talk about everything that's screwed up in the books category. Suffice it to say that for most items that you sell, your product MUST match the listing EXACTLY without one single difference.

• *Add pictures of alternate packaging.* If you sell a product that has lots of packaging variations like health and beauty, food or other consumable categories, add your picture to the listing rather than try to describe the difference in your condition notes. You may need to enlist Amazon's help if you did not originally create the listing. Show them the manufacturer's website, for example, where their new packaging is described, or another retailer's site where the alternate packaging is displayed. (By the way, this is <u>manufacturer's</u> packaging, not your re-packaging of a bulk purchase.) You will also want to add a note to the product description to the effect of: "Please note product packaging variations in pictures to the left."

• *Don't repackage and list on retail packaging.* If you have bought in bulk and re-packaged, you will need to create a new listing that shows your packaging. You see this with things like candy, baby formula and the like, where the seller has put a pound of loose candy into a polybag or 20 individual formula packets into a polybag. It must be clear to the consumer what to expect when they order the product. Watch out for new repackaging rules in the grocery category.

• *Make sure your products REALLY match.* Remember the story of my client who was putting helpful subtitle-removal instruction stickers on his DVDs? I also had a client who bought product from the manufacturer, which had decided to reuse a 30-serving bottle for 60 servings (or maybe vice versa). The manufacturer slapped a new sticker over the old one. One of my client's customers decided to peel off the new sticker and was convinced there was something fishy going on because of this sticker. Another client was selling a loose product without a retail box. While he technically matched the listing (which said nothing about a box one way or the other), customers complained he was selling counterfeit. They expected a retail box instead of a loose product in bubble wrap. Look at your listings and ask yourself if someone could possibly be confused or have an expectation you might not initially anticipate. In the case of the bottle with different serving quantities, my client didn't pay attention when the bottles came in. That is an easy fix for him from now on. Besides talking to the manufacturer, he is now more diligent when product arrives at his warehouse. For my client with the loose product, he now shrink wraps it before shipping.

- *Be honest in your description.* You'd think this would be obvious, but people are confused by the difference between marketing and telling the truth. OK, that was a trick statement. Marketing is <u>still</u> supposed to be the truth! While there are subjective terms like "delicious," be very careful with claims like weight loss, lowering cholesterol or raising your pecker. All the supplement guys I've ever worked with skated pretty close to the line of making claims the product can't support. If it is a cheap piece of plastic from China, don't say stuff like "high quality!" You are asking for trouble. If your product is a knockoff or a generic, and you sell it as the real thing, you are asking for instant banishment. This is serious business with Amazon. If you are selling on someone else's listing and really have no idea if your product is any good or actually matches the description (I see this often with people who source through retail arbitrage), don't sell it!

- *Comply with regulations.* Many people sell in regulated niches without knowing what they are doing. They may be buying a ton of great stuff at CVS and see other sellers up there and decide to sell as well. This can be a terrible mistake, especially if they miss the notices about new FDA rulings and restricted ingredients. They may add items to the catalog without being aware of what they can and can't say legally. They usually don't know when Amazon is wrong, either, and can't get reinstated on a listing that has been closed unnecessarily. Don't rely on the wisdom of the crowd in this case because those other sellers could be lemmings.

Supplements, over-the-counter drugs, cosmetics, personal-care products and some foods are the biggest danger areas. If you are going to sell in these categories, educate yourself. Don't send in inventory until you are confident that the ingredients are not restricted. Read every email you get from Amazon about new FDA findings or newly restricted ingredients. Since many FBA sellers don't have product on hand with an ingredients list to check, I suggest you add the ingredients to your listings as you join them. Take a high-quality picture of your ingredients and nutrition information (if relevant) and add it as a secondary picture to the listing. It will help your customers, and it will help you if there is ever a question about your product's ingredients. I give the same advice to MF sellers for a different reason: Ultimately Amazon is going to make you do it anyway, just like they did recently in food. You might as well start complying now.

- *Fix your categories.* Again, this is not worth the effort for only a few units. But if you plan to sell a product regularly, you should not only check for the most correct listing (if there are multiples), but also the right category. If your product is for pets but the ASIN is in Kitchen, then it needs to be fixed. As an added incentive, any effort you make to improve a listing counts positively toward you in the algorithm Amazon uses to decide who gets the Buy Box for that listing and for how long. Now for the stick. If you create a listing and put a product into the wrong category, and it is quite clear what the right category should be, then you will get a warning the first time and suspended the second. Don't put your candy in menswear or your dog collar in kitchen or your food item in beauty. You will get caught and warned. If you don't know where to put your backpack or some other ambiguous item, look at the intent of the product. Is it being sold to children going to school or a family that camps together? If you are really stumped, call Seller Support and ask to speak to a category expert. Lastly, the *Everything Else* category is horribly abused. If you have a product that truly does not fit into one of the hundreds of categories and sub-categories on Amazon, you are probably selling something forbidden or illegal. Do not use this category unless you are positive there is no other home for your product.
- *Delete/archive listings.* If you are not actively selling on a listing and don't plan to again in the near future, you need to get it out of your inventory

immediately. You don't want to get dinged over a product you don't even sell. I see it happen all the time. Sellers mistakenly think that if they have zero items to sell, they are fine. Not so. You need to officially delete (MF sellers) or close and archive (FBA sellers) that item. In that way, you tell Amazon you are not selling it and not planning to sell it again in the near future. If a rights-holder files an "inauthentic" or copyright infringement on an old listing of yours, you are safe because you closed it down. Otherwise, you'd have to go through all the trouble of dealing with the issue.

- _Read your listings._ This dings a lot of sellers – me included – because we have many ASINs and no time to read them all. If you use third-party software to list your items, you don't even see Amazon's description. Instead you see just the title and picture. Later you find out that you either listed against the wrong ASIN or that there are serious problems with your ASIN's description that need to be fixed before this listing goes live. Unfortunately, most of us find this out _after_ our listings are live. I suggest a multi-stage approach. Start with all your listings, replenishments etc., going forward. From now on, read your listings when you are preparing your inventory. For your older merchandise, either delegate or break it into manageable pieces – 20 a week, something like that. Besides general information, you want to check for:
  - _Multipacks_
  - _ASIN and picture changes_
  - _False claims_

STEP SIX: ADJUST YOUR POLICIES

Some of my clients have dreadful shipping and returns policies. They get in trouble constantly with their customers who want to know where their products are. Or, customers are getting the third degree from them when they want to return a product for a refund. The buyer complains to Amazon, who sides with them.

Sellers with these policies need to shift their mindset. Writing and posting a policy is not good enough. There has to be real change inside the company. If most of your customer complaints are caused by how you approach shipping and returns/refunds, you need to fix it now. Unhappy customers are not allowed in Amazon's world. Check your current policy against this list and see if there are any areas where you can improve:

Shipping. Here are the basic mistakes I see:

- No reliable tracking (hint: USPS is a poor partner) or no tracking at all. (I see that in the UK and overseas.)
- No email to the customer letting them know when their product is due.
- Poor packing/packaging.
- No insurance on your packages.
- Poor reimbursement policy by your carrier.
- Replacement units or missing parts are not sent by express mail.
- Doesn't take responsibility – points fingers at the carrier.
- Customers forced to go to post office or customs (overseas) to get their packages. What a hassle!

Returns/Refunds. The most common errors:

- Not automated/hard for the customer.
- Not responsive to customer inquiries/requests.
- Arguing with customers, insisting on pictures of the item in question and essentially calling the customer a liar and a cheat.
- Partial refund given instead of full.
- No pre-paid shipping label for returns.
- Doesn't use pre-written customer-service email templates.
- No real policy or procedure in place besides "no refunds after 30 days."
- Gets emotionally involved with the outcome.

A question I hope you are asking yourself at this point is, "Why am I in the shipping and customer-service business when I should be selling?" You can make things easier for yourself by turning on the automated returns setting and answering a couple of questions. It gives all your customers, whether they are FBA or MF customers, the ability to use the automated returns system at Amazon. With just a couple of clicks, they can print off their return shipping labels. Your number of inquiries about returns drops significantly.

If you have any ASINs that you want to be exceptions, you can tell Amazon you will handle those yourself.

You can boost your customer-service success by a series of emails. I've mentioned Feedback Genius before and will say here that simply letting customers know when a product is due and giving them a one-click solution to return their goods is very powerful. Don't make them go find their order; give them the direct link! That's what Feedback Genius does, and it is awesome. I include that link in *all* my emails to customers, even when I'm asking for feedback. You have to have the automated returns turned on; otherwise, the customer emails you for a return.

If a customer sends a product back, make sure the refund is processed *immediately* and send him an email letting him know a refund has been applied. If you are using Amazon to process your returns, they'll do this for you, of course.

If a customer complains about a missing part, a lost product or damaged merchandise, send her a part or replacement unit by express mail and let her know it is coming. Your responsiveness will make her very happy. I have a client who has a number of positive feedback "5" rating where the customer said, "The CD case was cracked when it came, but the seller sent me a new one by express mail for free!" They're thrilled.

STEP SEVEN: *CONSIDER FBA FOR PROBLEM ASINs*

Most shipping and performance problems can be resolved for a seller overnight by switching to FBA. For clients who are resistant to the idea (I had one guy who didn't want to have to downsize his warehouse crew), I suggest they at least switch some of their problem ASINs to FBA. A problem ASIN represents a product that is frequently damaged in shipping, routinely late for some reason, or has issues with theft/dishonest buyers.

I have one client right now who has lost dozens of units of a very expensive discontinued salon product because the buyers all claim never to have received the product. He sends, re-sends, re-sends and ultimately refunds. Now they have all these free units of shampoo. The UPS says the products are delivered, so they won't pay him for the lost product. Amazon sides with the customers, even though they know the buyers are liars. We suspect a team of geographically dispersed friends. The situation made my client very angry, and one vindictive buyer threatened him when he pointed out that the UPS guy remembered putting the package into her hands personally. She said, "You don't want me to make a claim with Amazon do you?" and basically had him over a barrel. We are going to turn her in once he is reinstated.

I convinced him to switch to FBA. Amazon will deal with the liars and reimburse him if the package is "lost" in shipping. He is out of the customer-service business, and it is good for him. He was becoming cynical and depressed.

Another client had such appalling customer-service instincts that I suggested he switch to FBA. His customers weren't just complaining. They were get-the-pitchforks-and-torches *outraged*. No amount of advice from me was going to fix this situation for him – he couldn't help himself. He was busy and tired and found his customers annoying. He is out of the customer-service business now.

One of my UK clients had committed so many "sins" with shipping that I knew he would never be reinstated if he didn't switch 100% to FBA and stop shipping product from the U.S. to the UK. He resisted it a lot and it came down to not wanting to figure out Value-Added Tax (VAT). Learning VAT is preferable to not selling at all, however. When someone writes the "1-2-3 Guide to VAT," I'll buy a copy for every one of my customers who ships to the UK or other European country from the U.S.

Obviously, FBA isn't the answer for everyone or every ASIN. If you sell furniture or large auto parts, for example, FBA would be insanely expensive.

STEP EIGHT: *DON'T SELL PRODUCT YOU DON'T OWN (DROP SHIPPING)*

I have met clients who have really excellent drop shipping partners. Great drop shipping arrangements are rare, and they didn't stop my clients from being suspended for drop shipping. To be clear, Amazon doesn't forbid drop shipping. When I say suspended for drop shipping, I mean all the potential problems with drop shipping: cancelled orders, late shipments, poor tracking, difficult returns, negative feedback, A-to-Z claims...you get the picture. And so does Amazon. If you are identified as a drop shipper by their robots, they'll come for you hard and they won't forgive. Amazon wants you to have the product in hand before you list it on Amazon. They want their customers to get their products fast, not a week or two from now, and they want easy returns.

You are putting your business in someone else's hands if you drop ship. I've seen it done right, but mostly I've seen it go horribly, horribly wrong. If you drop ship, look at your metrics and customer complaints – are you already in trouble?

Usually a small portion of your inventory generates the most sales. If you drop ship fast-selling items that aren't huge, consider buying a few cases and sending them in FBA instead of relying on your drop shipper. (I'm sure you are familiar with the concept of wholesale?) Amazon likes that better.

Recently, Amazon has forbidden retail drop shipping as a practice. This is a banishing offense now. In other words, don't list items on Amazon and then fulfill them from an online retailer like drugstore.com or Target.com.

STEP NINE: *PREPARE FOR COUNTERFEIT CLAIMS*

Customers claim all kinds of things in order to get free shipping, and some of them trigger the robots. Even if they aren't saying counterfeit, several "Does Not Match Description" claims back-to-back could have you looking at a counterfeit claim. If your listing is shut down or you are suspended for counterfeit, your best defense is to be prepared with the right invoices. If you look at your current inventory right now and think about where you bought it – are you vulnerable?

Good Enough

- Wholesalers
- Manufacturers
- Rights-holders
- Authorized resellers and distributors
- Major retailers IF receipts have full product name and UPC code

Not Good Enough

- Most online receipts
- Receipts without product name and UPC codes
- Liquidators

- eBay dealers
- Thrift stores, discounters and overstocks *unless* the UPC code and full name are included on receipt
- Products bought on Amazon and flipped

Seeing what I see every day has changed how I purchase inventory. It is about what you can prove, and you are guilty until proven innocent with Amazon. Since I started this consultancy practice, I now organize my receipts much better. They are all scanned and searchable. (I use ShoeBox.) I've stopped retail arbitrage and focus on wholesale. I'm less interested in liquidators or guys who sell large lots of things – even if it is a case of merchandise directly from Amazon – because they don't have detailed invoices.

STEP TEN: *IMPROVE YOUR EXAMINATION AND TESTING PROCESSES*

I see a lot of people who bought from liquidators suspended for "Used Sold as New" claims as well as counterfeit. Most liquidators include returns and repackaged goods in their lots that they sell you. If you sell those on Amazon as New, you're in trouble. Also, liquidation products tend to be scruffy with lots of shelf wear and dirt. It is such a big issue that Amazon has made it *THE* suspension reason for the past couple of weeks. Lots of sellers are dealing with "Used Sold as New" whether it is relevant to their case or not. For my clients who buy from liquidators, it is super important that they examine every item closely and have some kind of testing process if it is an electronic item. This means that a lot of their liquidation purchase will be sold Used.

Another thing I've seen catch sellers by surprise are manufacturers that change the packaging or add or subtract items from their normal packages without telling the buyer. These can be very minor things or big things. If you send in the inventory and it does not match the listing *exactly*, you are in trouble. You need an in-house process for catching changes before items are sold and shipped. It has to be:

- Easy
- Reliable

- Repeatable
- Effective

Among other things, you want to open a package and inspect the insides closely. You don't necessarily have to do this every time you send in a replenishment, but certainly every time you have a shipment from a new supplier you should look inside the box as well as outside. You can re-sell that unit Used or discard it. At least you will be confident that there are no missing parts.

One of our clients had a manufacturer that failed to include an instruction book in an entire lot of product. This ended up hurting my client because he hadn't examined the merchandise very closely before sending it to Amazon. Now he was dinged for "Missing Parts." Another client sold cell phones and the manufacturers were constantly changing what was in the package (besides the phone) like chargers, cords, etc., with no warning. From now on, he has to open a box from *every* shipment to check for problems because they change things so often. He has to create new listings, which is a hassle.

If you are accustomed to selling merchandise that is shipped from suppliers directly to Amazon, you might want to make sure you get a unit to examine first. Don't go live with your listing until you've examined it. This will help you spot problems before inflicting them on your customer. If you use Amazon to label/prep your inventory, they will send you a unit to examine. This will give you a chance to examine Amazon's packaging as well.

An important part of the appeal when you are suspended is the Plan of Action. The purpose of this Plan is to tell Amazon what you will do proactively to avoid the problem happening again. This is different from all the reactive things you are doing (recalling inventory, etc.) once you are suspended.

Because you are not currently suspended, this is your chance to be proactive. Make your Plan now about how to reduce complaints by better examining your inventory before it goes on sale. For people who source inventory through retail arbitrage, they have no one to blame but themselves if the customers are complaining about dinged, dirty and scruffy-looking inventory. Don't buy crap! Buy pristine products. It is not worth losing your business over one questionable box that you decided to send in instead of put back down. You have the receipt. Return it unless it is perfect, and then make sure you pack it very well so it gets to Amazon in perfect condition. This is your responsibility. These are factors you can control.

Wholesale and online arbitrage sellers are not off the hook for this, either. Make sure there is someone/a team in your process that is examining boxes when they come in. P.S. You can't count on Amazon. Not all of their warehouse teams are up to snuff. I strongly suggest a middle person between the supplier and Amazon that is examining inventory for you, if you are not examining it for yourself.

STEP ELEVEN: *COMMIT TO A BETTER CUSTOMER EXPERIENCE*

It seems obvious, but Amazon is crazy about the customer experience. It expects you to be, too. I'm often surprised at sellers who don't understand this. I've seen my clients argue with customers, call them names, be stingy with refunds and generally make it tough for anyone who dares to have a question or want a refund. To help stay out of Amazon's crosshairs, you need to look like them, act like them and take care of the customer like them.

The customer is not the enemy – even the liars, thieves and mischief-makers. If your business is not generating enough revenue to handle your returns as a small, manageable portion of your sales, you have a big problem with your financial model or products that you are selling. *That* is your enemy. Most businesses accept returns as part of doing business and can afford the losses.

If you are unhappy with your refund rate, then *YOU* need to do something about it. The problem isn't the customer. The problem is the product and how you are handling it. If, for example, you are making strong claims about your product, your product better back them up. If people are really mad when they are trying to get a return, try to find out why and *fix* it for them. You are their friend, not the enemy.

Two of my clients had regular complaints with several of their DVD products. Customers didn't like that the DVDs were subtitled. Why is that? Was it because they didn't know how to turn off the subtitles? Not really. Most people figured that out. They didn't like it because they felt tricked. The product wasn't what they expected. They worried about the quality. We started adding the word "foreign import" to the descriptions. We sent the customer instructions by email when the product arrived that told them how to remove the subtitles. We reassured them that we were buying our product directly from the manufacturer – just in another country.

It helped because my clients addressed the customer problem head-on. They didn't stand back and say, "Those stupid customers! They can't even figure out how to turn off their subtitles!" They didn't say, "If I point the problem out to them, my complaints will go up." They said, "There must be something I can do to make it easier for my customer." That is what sets the great sellers apart from the good ones. They take responsibility for every aspect of the sales process – even the customer's perceptions and reactions. Do they still get complaints about the subtitles? Yes, but a lot fewer than before.

Supplement sellers have a high rate of returns with their products because some people take them and don't lose weight, don't get stronger, aren't smarter, aren't more virile...you get the picture. They return products for "defective" because they get free shipping and because they are still fat, impotent, weak, dumb...and they hate that. They can't admit the problem might be their own behaviors or their inability to follow directions. No, it must be that the magic pills don't work. And yet, the better supplement sellers have higher positive feedbacks, fewer returns than standard and virtually no claims of "defective." How do they do that? They:

1.   Advertise that they offer no-hassle refunds as part of their returns policy.
2.   Offer refunds for 60, or sometimes 90, days.
3.   Deliver cheerful and immediate refunds.
4.   Give automated and FREE returns for the few who will return New, unopened items. (Maybe they ordered the wrong product by accident.)
5.   Tell customers there is no need to return the product. (They can't resell it anyway, most likely.)
6.   Ask for positive feedback right after issuing the refund.

I can hear the gasps now. Let me add that these are very *profitable, successful, high-volume sellers.* I don't want to get too "Christmas Carol" here, but greatness is rarely built on parsimony. It is built on generosity of spirit and passion. Step back and look at the big picture. Happy customers tend to come back and spend more. Customers who are unsure about buying will take the plunge if they feel safe doing so. Not all of them will return the product.

When you look at your returns report, what do you see? Unhappy customers? Are certain products responsible for a lot of the total returns? To avoid suspension, look at your account the way Amazon does. Think about their crazy commitment to their customers. Are your metrics reflecting your commitment? Take responsibility and take action. Fix those problem ASINs with high returns. Turn your customer's frowns upside-down.

Think of these as the 10 Amazon Commandments of Customer Service[6] and apply them to your business:

1. Fix The Customer's Problem – Make Everything Easy
2. Don't Cancel the Customer's Orders
3. Make Them Happy and Ask For Positive Feedback
4. Be a Refunder, Not a Fighter
5. Fix A-to-Z Claims Yourself
6. Shut Down Bad Products Fast
7. Improve Your Packaging
8. Find Better Shipping Partners
9. Don't Sell Poor-Quality Inventory
10. If Customers Complain, It's Too Late

STEP TWELVE: *GET AUTHORIZED*

For sellers who begin with retail or online arbitrage, this is a foreign concept. We are not authorized resellers of these products. We are not necessarily selling fake product, but we are not authorized. Because of that, there can be problems with our competitors, with manufacturers and sometimes with Amazon with claims of "inauthentic."

Some industries are more likely to have exclusive seller arrangements than others. You see this in industries and product lines that were traditionally sold through territories or select retail outlets like salons or doctors' offices or distributors. Do you think your house contractor buys his electrical components from Home Depot? No. That's for consumers. He buys them through distributors, where he can get the service and exact products that he needs for the job. The selection is ten times what you'll

6 Made up by me, to be clear. My understanding from the *New York Times* story is they have 14 principles they live by.

find in a retail hardware store. Electronics, car parts…the list goes on and on. The sellers of these business-to-business products usually own territories and have exclusive rights for those areas much like a franchise.

What happens when these products are now sold on Amazon? It is confusing and chaotic for the occasional seller, but the insiders know the score. Here are a few things you may not know about brands and territories on the platform:

1. There are two brand registries. One is for smaller sellers, and one is for big sellers that came to Amazon from the traditional background I mentioned above.

2. Getting registered in the first brand registry is what happens to the private label guys and the people who have product exclusives. They have ownership over their listing and their product, *but* other sellers can list on the listing. You have to defend it and kick off the interlopers. Still, at least you can do that.

3. In the second brand registry, the brand owner can create a secret list of approved sellers for its products such that only these approved sellers can list on that product. No muss, no fuss. The downside from the outside seller's point of view is that this list is secret. You will get shut down if you try to list on that product, and will not know why or have any recourse.

For my guys in electronics with high-volume sales, it is almost imperative to get approved to sell on certain listings. Someone will try to kick you off with policy violations, or claims of counterfeit, inauthentic, "Not as Described," or something else. Sellers might even come under attack from the manufacturer that wants to protect its relationships with its brick-and-mortar resellers. Usually a letter from the U.S. distributor or the manufacturer (or sometimes both) is required. If you can get your company's name put on the manufacturer's official list of resellers/distributors on their website, all the better.

In case you are wondering, you can get suspended for this issue, absolutely. Just ask Joly Stick. He fought hard to get authorized on several particular listings because his sales were worth more than $1 million a year on just one ASIN.

Getting authorized isn't required for everyone, of course, but it can pop up in the strangest ways. I have a client who sells high-end beauty products that are normally only available in high-end salons. Great niche, right? Well...there was a tiny hitch. The manufacturer will cut off and disavow forever anyone found violating its contract and selling its products online. When my client was accused of counterfeit, he was strangely reluctant to give his invoices to Amazon.

I was a little slow, but I figured it out after a few minutes. We threw out that Plan of Action and tried a completely different tack because I suddenly understood that it was most likely that the manufacturer who had filed against him was trying to flush out who had violated the sales agreement. My client would never get reinstated that way. The manufacturer would claim the invoices were "inauthentic" and that they did not sell to him. (This was technically true. They sold to his salon.) Selling against his agreement with the manufacturer was a mistake, but I felt badly for my client who paid a terrible price in laid-off employees who were like family to him and nearly $100,000 in funds held hostage by Amazon. He kept calling me on the phone and saying, "They are crying and crying to me! I need to know what is going to happen!" He cared about his employees a lot and paid them for weeks while we waited to hear back from Amazon.

If it makes sense for what you are selling, take the trouble to get authorized. If a competitor is kicking you off a listing, you MUST get authorized. If you are selling product you know is against your contract with another company (that includes all you MLM people who are selling off old inventory online), you are vulnerable to vengeance from the rights-holder.

Another group that might want to think about getting authorized are *suppliers* of goods to third-party sellers. As I've mentioned previously, Amazon is opposed to certain sources of inventory. If you are a distributor, wholesaler or liquidator and not officially authorized by the manufacturer to sell the goods you are selling, it could be a problem down the road. If your invoices are the ones that Amazon is rejecting, you will lose business from Amazon sellers.

One thing you can do to help your customers that are Amazon sellers is to have detailed, itemized invoices with UPC codes and product names. Take the call, also, if Amazon wants to verify your inventory sources.

STEP THIRTEEN: *STOP COUNTERFEIT*

This is for all of you who buy cheap goods from Alibaba and China in general. If you are selling a generic product, you are probably fine as long as it is not infringing on someone else's intellectual property. If you are selling a licensed product, be very careful. You need to thoroughly check your partners out and make sure Disney isn't going to breathe down your neck for illegally using its princesses, for example.

Before its IPO in 2014, Alibaba took down 90 million (yes, million) fake product listings. That should tell you something. Do you think those 90 million sellers all went away meekly, or did they create a new name and sign up again? That's right. There are plenty of bad operators still up there.

There's a lot of talk about Chinese sites like AliExpress being hotbeds of counterfeit product sales, but an even larger amount of counterfeit goods is sold on eBay. More complaints come from eBay customers about unwittingly buying a counterfeit product than from customers on any other platform in the world. If you do a fair amount of eBay arbitrage for products to sell on Amazon, do your homework or you might be bringing counterfeit goods into your Amazon portfolio unintentionally. If you are ever accused of counterfeit, you will not be able to defend yourself. The eBay seller is not going to help you out. Amazon will reject your receipt.

One way to stay out of trouble is to not sell DVDs or luxury goods, as those are the most frequent offenders. If it seems too good to be true, it probably is. That being said, I've seen some pretty crazy counterfeit things that you wouldn't expect, like baking soda. You are naturally suspicious of cheap watches, but laundry detergent? There is a whole world of legitimate merchandise out there that should sell on Amazon perfectly fine without any problems. How do you protect yourself from counterfeit goods and find the good stuff?

How to detect counterfeit is a book by itself. I've written blog posts that only scratched the surface of the topic. There is, however, a protective shortcut. I suggest a "two strikes and you're out!" policy. If one customer complains about counterfeit or quality, take it seriously. Have the product returned and take a good look at it and make sure this is the product you sent in (there are dishonest buyers as well as sellers). If a second customer complains, shut it all down immediately and start preparing your defense. Close/suspend your listings and decide what you want to do. If you are confident that your product is legit, then pull your invoices together and get ready to defend them. If you've been diligent up front, this should be easy to do. If you are not sure and want to avoid trouble before it gets on Amazon's radar, remove your inventory and demand a refund from the manufacturer/supplier. (Don't hold your breath on this – dishonest players don't refund.) Make sure that counterfeit claim isn't really about damage in shipping or a related claim.

If Amazon comes to you about counterfeit, you can tell them you already took action when you saw your customers' concerns and show your steps.

Send emails to your customers asking them why they think it is counterfeit and make sure you get their merchandise back to examine for yourself. Of course you are going to refund their money *and* pay for the return shipping. Because this issue is so serious, I recommend calling your customer if you can't reach them by email. (Email first, though.) Be friendly, helpful and curious.

One client had received several complaints about a particular product not being new. He was bewildered by this because he was buying from an authorized distributor. He found out just in time that the manufacturer had disavowed that distributor and severed its business relationship with it for packing up returns and selling them as New. By providing Amazon with the manufacturer's letter to its reseller community disavowing the distributor, my client was reinstated. This is another example of why buying from legitimate sources is so important. My customer was buying from what was an authorized reseller. He would not have been reinstated if he hadn't been.

Another client lost her selling privileges completely because she had several counterfeit complaints one right after the other in a short time period. She didn't respond quickly enough and was banned. We are still working on her case. Be fast. Don't let a potentially counterfeit product keep selling on the platform.

You should also check out your partners before you buy from them. Some sellers got in trouble for using a category ungating service to get them into DVDs. By turning the whole process over to someone else, they were vulnerable to that person's/company's mistakes. And this was a doozy. To get ungated requires that you tell Amazon at least two sources you will buy from. One of the sources chosen by this ungating company for its clients was a liquidator. Dozens of sellers had this company listed as a source, and many of them actually ordered from this source.

A few seconds on that liquidator's website and I knew they were trouble. Not only were they a liquidator, which is NOT an authorized reseller, but they also clearly took no steps to make sure their product was legitimate. They were based in China. They didn't disclose their sources. In Amazon's world, buying from these guys was as bad as buying it off a blanket in Times Square or a street box in Chinatown. So why did Amazon approve all those sellers in DVDs? It was a different Amazon department. The Amazon gated category approvers are different from the Amazon policy violation group. Eventually the policy violation guys caught up and they punished the ungating company, as well as the sellers who used them.

Whose fault was this? That's right. It was the sellers' fault. The ungating company bears some measure of blame, too, but it is *your* account at risk here. You are responsible. While it is OK to get help with your business, *you* need to look at the application and approve it. *You* need to be the one who posts it to Seller Central. If you don't know enough about Amazon's requirements to judge the quality of your vendor's submission, *you* need to learn. There is really no shortcut to getting into an ungated category. Even if you hire a service, you still need to know how the category works or you'll get suspended for violating a category rule down the road. The whole idea of the ungating process is to teach sellers how to be successful in the category.

If this story isn't sufficiently chilling yet, I will tell you that sellers who bought from that Chinese company were banned *for life*. Their invoices were not approved. They were out. I got two sellers reinstated by throwing themselves on Amazon's mercy and begging for another chance. They promised to never sell in DVDs again. They removed or destroyed their DVD inventory. We sent the letter directly to Jeff Bezos' people. Amazon waited more than two months to reinstate them. They were *punished* and put on probation, but they were forgiven. Other sellers weren't so lucky.

STEP FOURTEEN: *PRACTICE SAFE SELLING*

It amuses me to think of commingling as an Amazon social disease – particularly since the solution is to wear a prophylactic aid (aka an FNSKU label). It is not funny in practice, however. Sellers are highly vulnerable to the integrity of other sellers when they commingle.

Anyone who sells New FBA items is technically a commingler. Amazon may take a product from another seller, send it to your customer, and then use your product to resupply that other seller's stash. The reason they do this, of course, is to get product quickly to the customer. If you don't have any inventory in a California warehouse, but your fellow seller does, they'll take his and then ship yours to that warehouse to replenish it. They might even send several units to that warehouse if they think there will be a lot of demand in California. Somewhere in the black box that is Amazon, they keep track of these things. Most of the time it works pretty well.

The official commingler is the seller that sends in her inventory "stickerless commingled." This means she doesn't have labels on her product. The units go into a big pool of available units, which are used interchangeably to meet customer demand. In theory this is a great idea for the seller, for Amazon, and for the customer. In practice, it leads to danger and tears.

It goes wrong when your fellow sellers are careless (at best) or unethical. They bring counterfeit or scruffy inventory into the pool of products. They are the proverbial bad apples. Your customer received this horror and complains against you. You have to prove to Amazon that your inventory is good, and it wasn't you. The unhappy customer is still *yours* even if Amazon agrees with you that your product was bought from a reputable source. (Your product *was* bought from a reputable source, right?) Now you are paying the price for someone else's treachery.

Why doesn't this happen to the guys who sell regular FBA if they are unofficially comminglers? Because they have an FNSKU sticker on the back of their products. Amazon knows they are not the bad apple. Their customer may be upset, but it is possible to prove to Amazon that it wasn't their inventory. All they have to do is look at their black box. Amazon will support them and even reimburse them if it was Amazon's fault for shipping someone else's inventory to the customer. It is the least Amazon can do.

The solution for the stickerless commingled sellers is to have Amazon sticker their products – or to do it themselves. It currently costs 20 cents a unit for Amazon to put a label on your product. Think of it as insurance. If 20 cents per unit eats into your profits too much, you have another problem to deal with – your margins. Your inventory will still be sold commingled, but you are protected if the faulty product isn't yours. It also makes it a lot easier for Amazon to track down the bad actor by process of elimination.

Remember when Amazon shut down all Disney *Frozen*® products and required sellers to get approved to sell *Frozen* goods? That was because the counterfeit problem was so bad and they had so many stickerless comminglers that they couldn't track the bad apples. Everyone's inventory had to be examined. Everyone had to be re-approved. Many sellers weren't. Amazon lost a lot of money because of this. They had to throw out the bad inventory and still make their sellers whole. Their customers were unhappy because Amazon alone could not keep up with the demand and frequently sold out of popular goods. This was a case where Amazon's stickerless commingling idea came crashing down around them.

And yet my clients still often resist the idea of labeling their products. We usually compromise by having them label the problem ASINs to start. It is a stop-gap measure. They are still practicing highly risky selling. Unless you are the ONLY provider of a product on Amazon, you are risking everything you have when you stickerless commingle.

Some may be thinking, "I have great invoices, so I don't need to worry." OK, maybe you don't need to worry about being *reinstated*, but you do have to worry about being *suspended*. The robots do that. Right now it is taking more than three weeks for some of our customers to get reinstated *after* they turn in their Plans. Considering our backlog, it can easily take five business days to get a Plan written. That's three weeks you are not selling. What is that worth to you? Is it worth 20 cents a unit? Some of our clients come to us with only days left before their 17-day Plan of Action deadline with Amazon. We charge them more to expedite their Plans (we have to work all night), so that's thousands of dollars in our fees, plus their losses, plus Amazon is still likely to hold on to part or all of their money for a week to a month once they are reinstated while Amazon conducts an in-depth review of the sellers' business. OK. End of lecture.

STEP FIFTEEN: *MANAGE YOUR PARTNERS*

I've said it throughout this book, but you are responsible for your business. It is OK to use outside services and to have partners in your business that help you manage inventory, reprice your goods, prepare inventory for fulfillment, get you into ungated categories, etc. What you can't do is take your eye off the situation because you are still ultimately responsible for the end result. Just like you still need to learn about Amazon's category requirements, you also need to make sure your partners are reputable and doing their jobs.

I've had clients explain to me how a technology snafu messed up their orders or tracking or caused them to cancel an order. I get it, but my question back is always, "How are you going to make sure it never happens again?" This usually is more difficult because my clients are not used to looking at their business that way. They are used to dealing with the problem then moving on to the next issue.

Amazon sees that as reactive and not proactive. They are a continuous improvement organization. This is how the proactive approach looks in practice. My client had a problem because he accidentally uploaded the previous day's shipments again to Amazon. It created a big mess. I said, "OK, we can explain that to Amazon. Now, how are you going to make sure that doesn't happen again?" Silence. It was human error, and he didn't know how to prevent that from happening again. Everyone makes mistakes.

I pushed back, examining every step of how the problem had occurred. I learned that he gets the spreadsheets from his shipping partner by email every day. He had accidentally chosen the wrong email and hastily uploaded it. He would be more careful in the future. "Not good enough for Amazon!" I said. More silence.

"How about if you add two new steps to your process?" Now after he uploads the spreadsheet every night, he saves the file to his hard drive, and he deletes the email from his shipping partner. That's it. Assuming he follows his procedure, he can never choose the wrong email again because it won't be there. I suggested he stick a note to his computer screen until the procedure became routine. In addition, he needed to make sure that any new person he trained followed the same procedure. Maybe a short checklist taped to the side of the screen would be helpful.

That is the difference between a reactive plan and a proactive plan. A reactive plan fixes the current mess. A proactive plan avoids a future mess. When you make mistakes in your business or problems come up, you need to take time after the mess is fixed to figure out how to avoid it happening in the future. Most businesses do this for really painful problems (i.e. cost money, took an emotional toll). You need to do it for ANY problem that affects your operations with Amazon.

Your solution does not have to be elaborate, expensive or time-consuming. It just needs to be effective and thought through. My client was reinstated. We detailed his new procedure, and Amazon liked it. He showed he can think like them.

Another client had a big issue with a third-party software vendor that messed up inventory numbers among platforms (he sold on eBay and other platforms besides Amazon), so he ended up with a lot of cancelled orders. He was perfectly happy to blame his software vendor, but had done nothing to make sure the problem didn't happen again. He thought that was out of his area of influence. He was wrong. He needed to address future problems *right away*. This was serious! He needed to sit down with his supplier and push them until he was confident the problem would not happen again – whatever it took. He was paying them a lot of money. This was unacceptable and a breach of contract. It had cost him money and time, and now he was suspended. How were they going to reimburse him for that?

I lit a fire under him, and he lit a fire under his software vendor, so that he could come back to Amazon with a clear Plan of Action that showed he had taken the initiative with his vendor to make sure the problem never happened again. I also learned that he was not 100% confident in how to use the vendor's software. It is possible part of the problem was from him or his team not using the tool properly. What was he going to do about that? They are all getting additional training now. I made it clear to him that someone at his business needed to *master* this program (so they could teach the others), and he also needed to know it very well – well enough to spot problems before they occurred.

Amazon understands tech problems, but they need to see solutions. I've had other clients who switched vendors when one of their partners failed them because they didn't have confidence the problem wouldn't happen again. They would have never known that if they hadn't pressed the vendor for answers and questioned their processes. I'm not saying you have to turn into Total Quality Management (TQM) fanatics, but you need to understand that your partner Amazon *is* a TQM fanatic.

THESE ARE THE KEY PRINCIPLES OF TQM[7]:

Management Commitment

- Plan (drive, direct)
- Do (deploy, support, participate)
- Check (review)
- Act (recognize, communicate, revise)

---

7 Martin, L. (1993). "Total Quality Management in the Public Sector," *National Productivity Review*, 10, 195-213.

Employee Empowerment

- Training
- Suggestion scheme
- Measurement and recognition
- Excellence teams

Fact-Based Decision-Making

- SPC (Statistical Process Control)
- DOE (Design of Experiments), FMEA (Failure Modes Effect Analysis)
- The 7 statistical tools
- TOPS (Team-Oriented Problem Solving)

Continuous Improvement

- Systematic measurement and focus on CONQ (Continuous Quality)
- Excellence teams
- Cross-functional process management
- Attain, maintain, improve standards

Customer Focus

- Supplier partnership
- Service relationship with internal customers
- Never compromise quality
- ***Customer-driven standards***

I include this list not to explain it – there are entire books dedicated to TQM – but to show you what you are up against when you have Amazon as a partner. They do know what this all means and they live it. In the recent *New York Times* story (http://bitly.com/InsideAmazonNYT), you can see how Amazon has pushed some of these principles to the extreme. "Excellence teams" sounds awesome until you realize it means forced firings annually to clear out the so-called deadwood. Amazon has taken measurement to a level never even imaginable by the original TQM authors. Time will tell if it is a good thing.

Of these principles, the last one – customer-driven standards – describes Amazon perfectly. When you ever wonder what to do or how to behave, ask yourself, "What is in the best interest of the customer?" That's what Amazon does. TQM is usually associated with large organizations like Amazon or Ford, and no one expects a small seller with a dozen employees (or just one employee) to operate the same way as the big guys. You can expect more, however: more from your partners, more from your suppliers and more from yourself.

When there is a problem, be sure to reflect later on how to prevent it from happening again. Think through all the steps in a non-judgmental, fact-finding way. See if any of those steps can be modified or adjusted. Remember the end goal is customer satisfaction.

Sometimes the problem arises from something that is so inherent in the person running the business that it can't be changed or fixed easily – if at all. I've had clients that I insisted needed to switch to FBA because I knew it would be next to impossible for them to make the changes needed to meet Amazon's exacting standards. The solution was to turn it over to a trustworthy partner: Amazon. And by the way, this was by no means an "easy button" solution. These clients' ability to learn and manage FBA was going to be challenging too. However, I recognized that their chances of success were better in the long-run with FBA.

When we write our clients' Plans, we follow TQM principles. We speak to Amazon in language it understands. We show our clients taking TQM steps to improve. We focus on the experience of *Amazon's customers*. We have our clients make real process changes in their businesses. This is why, when asked, I say we are not letter-writers, and why I don't review or edit letters written by people who have not gone through *my* process. I'm not interested in writing a great letter that tricks Amazon into reinstating my clients. I'm interested in making sure my clients never need me again.

You can do the same thing for yourself without having to learn a lot of jargon or read *Harvard Business Review*. Reflect on past mistakes and problems. Think about what happened and what you might do differently – real, actionable steps – to change it. Remember that the best way to not make a mistake is to eliminate the possibility of a mistake. The client who deleted his daily email after he was done with it could never make that particular mistake again.

Did you send the wrong product to a customer? Everyone has at some point. How do you stop that from happening again? If you are a small operation, then make sure your solution is realistic within the parameters of your resources and personality. Don't create a plan or process that you know you won't follow because you hate checklists or whatever. The nice thing about small operations is that you can arrange your universe to suit yourself.

If you are good at one part of your company operations but not another, think about how you can delegate operations in which you are weak and focus on those where you are strong. I'm not saying to improve your weakness areas – that's not really realistic – but to focus on your areas of strength. Figure out what you are really good at. Find a way to delegate the rest through partners, employees or whatever it takes. Someone or some other entity will be much better in areas where you are weak. Let it go. Your company will be better. You will be happier.

REINSTATEMENT NOTES:

- There is a lot that you can do *before* you are suspended to prevent it.
- The first thing you need to fix is your mindset. You are responsible...and you are empowered.
- Read your imperfect orders, negative feedback, returns reports and customer messages regularly. Then act on them.
- Check your inventory against the listing on Amazon. Read it. Look at the picture. Make sure your product matches *exactly*.
- Fix your listings to avoid customer confusion.
- Get authorized, if necessary.
- Examine your inventory before it gets to Amazon. Somewhere in your process there needs to be a person examining your inventory against a checklist of possible problems.
- Commit to a better customer experience and take action if your policies and procedures need work. Create templates. Make it easy for the customer to get a return/refund.

- Prevent counterfeit in your inventory and make sure your invoices are ready for examination if Amazon wants to see them.
- Don't sell product you don't own. If it isn't in your warehouse or Amazon's warehouse, you don't own it.
- You are vulnerable to counterfeit claims if you buy from liquidators and poor performance metrics if you buy from drop shippers.
- Sticker your inventory.
- Don't put your business success in anyone else's hands. You are the boss.
- Delegate in areas where you are weak, focus on areas where you are strong.

Part III

Get Clean, Stay Clean

7

Get Clean, Stay Clean

It would be reasonable to conclude by this point that avoiding suspension is work. You need to identify problems in your organization, fix them and then figure out how to keep them from happening again. Rinse and repeat.

The thing about change and improvement is that it is a process. No one gets clean overnight, and no one goes forward without making a mistake again. It happens. In the Suspension Prevention section we talked about specific issues that lead to suspension and how to fix them. That is your triage list for getting clean. Most sellers find a few things that they could improve upon from those 15 steps. Their first few weeks to months after reinstatement are all about cleaning things up.

We get rid of negative feedback, develop new customer-service policies and procedures, and generally execute the Plan we gave Amazon. Things get better. Once everything is in good shape and we are out of crisis mode, there is no time to coast. It is just like housekeeping. You can't clean the kitchen only once.

This chapter is about that dull topic: maintenance. In the beginning, something new is exciting and challenging. Then it can get kind of monotonous. All you drama queens out there know what I'm talking about. For this reason, I suggest keeping your interest piqued by focusing on a different best-business-practice area each month. See if you can identify a new action to take. Check in with Amazon to see if any of their processes have changed which might require you to change. Do a deep-clean on a particular business practice. To keep the analogy going, you have to clean your house regularly, but the window and closet-cleaning only have to be done once or twice a year.

BEST BUSINESS PRACTICES

1. Review your reports regularly
2. Respond fast
3. Don't let anything stand idly by
4. Take care of your customer
5. Always be learning
6. Run your business like Amazon would
7. Never cancel orders
8. Watch your pricing
9. Train your people
10. Buy quality product

<u>Review Your Reports Regularly.</u> At Online Sales Step by Step, we are big believers in looking at reports regularly. Big companies with lots of transactions should be reviewing the reports, customer messages and performance notifications weekly for patterns and signs of potential future problems. Smaller businesses may find that monthly is sufficient. As part of our *Get Clean Stay Clean* service, we prepare the "Canary Report." It tells clients what requires their attention <u>now</u> based on their reports and customer messages. If we start to see activity on an ASIN or an increase in types of complaints, we warn them.

A source within Amazon has told us that you get five hard hits a year and an unspecified number of soft hits to your account. Only five! This is not based on percentages, this is an absolute number. It is critical to stay on top of your reports and to close down problem ASINs quickly until you understand what is causing a spike in returns, etc.

Being aware is one of the first and easiest best practices to implement, and yet most of our clients were not doing it until we started working together. Now they do. It goes a long way towards helping them avoid being suspended again. For once-a-year housekeeping in this practice, we recommend examining all of Amazon's reports and determining what else should be reviewed regularly. Is there some historical data that can be reviewed for better performance? Are there additional reports that should be added to the "Canary Report?"

Respond Fast. Responding quickly is a given, but what does it mean to respond quickly? Is it within an hour? A day? A week? That is an internal metric for your company to determine based on your internal resources. There are a surprising number of parts and activities around "respond quickly." First is detection. How do you know there is something you need to respond to quickly? Slow detection can lead to slow response. Once you've identified something that requires a response – whether it is an Amazon notice or a customer complaint – then you need to figure out how long it is currently taking and why. Is there any room for improvement? Set a baseline of how things are done now and a goal of how you'd like things to be in the future. It may be that this activity requires a dedicated owner – someone whose job it is to make sure responses are fast. Give yourself time to get this process just right. Don't be like one of those crazy people who goes on a diet, joins a gym and buys a wardrobe of workout clothes on the same day. Pick one thing. Master it. Move on.

OK, OK. I know you are falling asleep on me, and I promised this was a way to make staying clean more interesting! Apply your brilliant business mind to the problem, and I promise it will be interesting in its own way. You are a natural problem-solver or you wouldn't be in business.

To be fast, you have to take action. I am often surprised how many of my clients sat idly by while Amazon sent them warning after warning, or their metrics got worse and worse. Don't sit idly by! It only gets worse. Amazon sometimes sends out messages and says, "There's no need to respond." That is a lie. You should respond. They've just brought a problem to you. What they mean is, "Don't pester us with questions." What I recommend my clients do is to fix the issue and then report the results to Amazon:

"Thank you for letting us know about issue X. We looked into it and took the following actions [1-2-3] to make sure it does not happen again. We wanted to let you know. Please notate our account. Sincerely..."

Don't Let Anything Stand Idly By. Not standing idly by also means taking action on other fronts. Remember my client who was approached by a competitor wanting her to raise her prices? This was dumb on his part, but also risky on hers. If she didn't say something about it, it was possible that he could have claimed later that she tried to price-fix with him. Evil persists while good men do nothing. Don't stand idly by while bad apples wreak havoc on all of us. It is morally wrong, and it is against everyone's best interests.

Let me add, while you are following best business practices, don't forget to look inside. I hate to say it, but you need to be diligent with your business, not just Amazon's. A former colleague of mine who was a turnaround CEO used to tell me about embezzlers and how they would steal hundreds of thousands to millions of dollars from their employers. They got away with it almost every time and went somewhere else – without a negative reference or anything – and they did it again. Why wouldn't they? He always strongly encouraged his clients to prosecute, but they rarely did. They were embarrassed. They were afraid of how it might affect their stock and/ or employees if anyone else found out. They were mortified at how long it had gone on before it was discovered. The company founder usually replaced the money out of his/her personal account.

Walter Ashes felt like his last name. His whole world was going up in smoke. First someone stole his login and tried to steal his next Amazon payment distribution. He was so grateful to Amazon for detecting the fraud on his account and helping him to change his password. He bought a new computer, as well as state-of-the-art malware and spyware detection. He took the Amazon Seller App off his phone. Then it happened again! Once again Amazon warned him…only they decided to also ban him for life from selling on Amazon. He had now been victimized by a shadowy person and Amazon. There was no friendly phone call from Amazon this time.

Amazon's fraud-prevention group will tell you most account breaches and money stolen from Amazon's accounts are an inside job – meaning someone inside your company is being dishonest with your account. Amazon can track the IP address and see exactly when and where it happened. If you don't fix the problem immediately, they ban *you*. This is horribly unfair, but you can see from their perspective why they can't trust you to maintain best practices or to look out for their best interests if you can't fix this issue inside your own business. The smart embezzlers change your notification email address first, so you don't notice when they change the bank for your funds transfer to an off-shore bank. Amazon will raise the red flag. They expect you to charge into action.

When you conduct your annual review of "idly by," brainstorm all the things you might be overlooking, ignoring or discounting the importance of in your business with things that seem like they are not a big deal, ask instead, "What if this was the biggest problem in my business? How would I address it? What would I want to do?"

<u>Take Care of Your Customer.</u> This is multi-faceted. In the beginning, most sellers focus on customer service, since that is what probably got them into trouble in the first place. This involves their policies, their scripts to the customer, how they address complaints, how they get positive feedback and much more. I promise you, this area of best practices is always interesting because of how customer complaints change. When your customers tell you something, you need to listen. It often indicates bigger issues than refunds. What they are telling you, for one thing, is that there was a problem you didn't proactively prevent. Once the customer complains, it is too late. You can't take back the negative experience. All you can do is learn from it.

Here's a real-world example. I received several cases of a food product where some of it was shattered in the boxes. Liquid was everywhere. My unbroken product was a mess and would need to be hand washed. I was upset at my supplier. When I looked closely, I saw that in one case the jar wasn't broken, but the lid had popped off. I instantly decided that I was not going to source from this supplier again, and I wanted my money back.

The lid popping off told me that the jars were not properly sealed, which means I could have a botulism factory in front of me. They were not vacuum-sealed or shrink wrapped, so I concluded the supplier was small-time, inexperienced and a huge risk for me. It's too bad. The food, when I tasted it at the gourmet food show, was delicious. I called my supplier and told her specifically:

1. The packaging was inadequate. It was double-boxed, but there was very little padding between the boxes and only a handful of Styrofoam peanuts.
2. The jars were not properly sealed, so she was at risk for making a customer sick.

3. The product could not be shipped back to her in the same boxes because they were soaked with product and useless.
4. The pictures I took would help her file a claim with FedEx®, *but* I did not personally think it was FedEx's fault. It was her fault for not packing the product properly.

I was very glad I had decided to have a small shipment sent to me first for examination instead of going directly to my packers. I don't know if she'll appreciate it or not, but that is some highly valuable intelligence for her from a customer. She lost me as a customer because of the safety thing, but she can fix everything for her future customers if she cares to listen to what I told her. Most Amazon customers aren't that helpful. You need to read between the lines. Sometimes you need to ask them more questions to figure out what is really going on – especially if you see patterns with certain ASINs. Be sure to take care of Amazon's customers first, and then try to learn from them. Customers are much more generous and thoughtful after their needs have been met.

<u>Always Be Learning.</u> This is a fun one for me personally. I see it as an opportunity to step away from the day-to-day of my business and learn something new that will make my business better. You are doing that now by reading this book. The goal here is to learn more about Amazon and its practices and to incorporate best practices into your business. You should also read Amazon's policies at least once a year to remind yourself of everything. If you've entered new categories, you'll especially want to make sure you know the rules. While you will be learning all year round as things come up, once a year at least it is a good idea to do some research into ideas that will make your business better.

<u>Run Your Business The Way Amazon Would.</u> How does Amazon run its business? Answering that question should keep you busy for a few years. They are the gold standard for online retail sales. I'm not saying to run your business like a huge business. I'm saying you should consider what is important to Amazon and incorporate those things into your business too. We all know that customer service and making things easy for the customer is important to Amazon. What can you do in your business to make it easy for the customer? We already talked about how continuous improvement is important to Amazon. How can you make sure that you are continuously improving? This exercise is a great start.

<u>Never Cancel Orders.</u> This is bad in Amazon's world. Cancelled orders indicate problems with inventory management, possible drop shipping and more. Don't make the mistake of one of my clients who would cancel orders because her customer asked her to. Never do that! Help customers cancel their own orders or get Amazon to help them cancel their orders. It counts heavily against you. Some businesses have trouble with this, and some don't. I'm all FBA so it isn't a problem for me. For MF sellers, it can be a big headache. When you look at the issue of "Never Cancel Orders," you need to examine all the factors that could possibly lead to you cancelling an order and then eliminate the possibility for a mistake to be made. If you have a lot of cancelled orders in your account, at least it will be easy to track your improvement.

<u>Watch Your Pricing.</u> Beyond repricing your inventory to stay competitive, you need to watch your pricing to keep your margins up and to avoid taking a loss. Keep an eye on your tools and make sure you don't reprice yourself into the poorhouse. Test your pricing so you know what your sweet spot is for sales and overall value. I love Feedvisor for this. That software program allows me to set rules, and then it reprices within them. It will price my item high and then drop it over time to find the sales sweet spot. Amazon is sensitive to screams of price-gouging from its customers, so it always encourages its sellers to go low, low, low. Try not to listen to that. We need to make money to pay all of Amazon's fees. Your goal is to find a price point at which you have good sales at a profit.

<u>Train Your People.</u> By this I don't mean train them in their jobs. I mean to train them in every aspect of the business. At Amazon, they move their employees around regularly so they can learn new things and get better and better. Your organization is smaller, so it is actually easier to teach your employees all aspects of the business over time. This gives you flexibility in your business and allows people (like you!) to take vacations and have life events without disrupting the business.

Training means they do the job correctly, the way it should be done. Training means they are learning new things, which keeps them interested in the job. Training means you can iron out the kinks in your internal processes and make them better. Training means you step back from the day-to-day of working the business to learn about making the business better through your people.

<u>Buy Quality Product.</u> Why is this on a list of best business practices? Shouldn't it be obvious? Apparently it isn't. Let's reflect back on all the issues Amazon has with

Used sold as New, counterfeit, Does Not Match Description and faulty products. Plenty of my clients had problem products in their inventory. They bought from shifty sources or they bought faded, scruffy-looking product and tried to pass it off as new. They relied on suppliers who let them down. They sold crappy products and wondered why customers complained.

I would add to this: buy product in categories that you know. I had one client who was selling everything from TVs to electronics to beauty products, but he really only knew the beauty marketplace. The other products were things he was selling for friends, and they got him suspended. He did not know what he was doing and got tons of complaints from the TV purchasers because of how hard it was to deliver the product to their homes when they could be there. All the logistics overwhelmed him. The electronics products were faulty because he didn't know to inspect and test them.

There is nothing wrong with expanding into new categories, but make sure you understand their quirks and challenges. Food has issues with expiration, packaging and listing. There are tons of rules around listing and what you can bundle, what you can multipack, etc. Electronics are better if you are authorized. Books...don't get me started about rules and quirks. I teach classes on books, and I still struggle to make the topic understandable in two hours.

At heart, whatever the category, you need a quality product. All the great practices and procedures in the world won't stop customers from complaining if the product is shoddy. There is no need to sell cheap, flimsy stuff to make money. You can make money with nice products that customers love to receive. A really great appliance is a joy forever. Cute Disney outfits that make you giggle when you buy them – awesome! If your inventory looks like it came from a bargain basement, it is time to upgrade your inventory. Make it a goal to change out your inventory to things you can be proud of *and* that make you money. That's a best practice that will help keep you safe from suspension.

PAY ATTENTION!

Almost all of my clients got suspended by Amazon because they weren't paying attention. They didn't realize the notices they were getting from Amazon were important. They didn't examine the reports that would have told them that they had a problem.

They are not bad sellers; they are certainly not lazy or stupid. Many of them are running huge seller operations – several with more than $1M a month in net revenue from Amazon. That's a lot of sales to track.

Why didn't they pay attention? Because they were busy, or they thought their employees were on top of it, or they simply didn't know what information was available to them. Recently, a seller asked me how I knew all the stuff I did about Amazon, and I told her a lot of it was in Seller Central. She was genuinely shocked. She didn't even realize that she could have negative feedback removed through the automatic system. She was making money and thought things were OK. It never occurred to her to really dig in and look around.

It took me more than a year to figure out Seller Central. If I hadn't had a blog, I would never have delved as deeply as I did into the reports and Help and all the thousands of pages of information Amazon gives us. My readers kept asking me questions, so I went to Amazon to get the answers. I can see how a busy seller can lose sight of what's going on in her account. Some of Amazon's stuff is obviously written by a lawyer and is incomprehensible to regular people.

You are a different seller now than before you picked up this book. You understand now how important it is to pay attention. Like many of my reinstatement clients, I hope that you, too, will make meaningful changes in your business going forward. Just paying attention and acting on what Amazon tells you will be a big help to you.

STAND ON YOUR FEET

Because so much of this book focuses on avoiding suspension, it might sound like I'm saying the customer is always right and that you have to slavishly do everything the customer wants. As one client put it to me, "I might as well just give away the product for free. It seems no one cares if I make money at this gig or not." It sure can seem that way sometimes, but it isn't true. Amazon wants us to make money – it is how they make money. It is our job to deal with the reality of selling on *their* platform.

People have asked me about my reinstatement Plans and if part of our success is groveling. Absolutely not! My clients stand on their feet. They've made mistakes and they own them, but they don't debase themselves. Their Plans of Action are about change and growth, not shame. They are genuinely sorry and realize the best way to show it is to fix the problem. Think about it, what kind of partner does Amazon want? Does *anyone* want? They want a partner they can respect and trust. They want someone who learns from their mistakes and focuses on being better.

The tone of our letters is always respectful and polite. We express regret and our desire to improve our relationship with Amazon and its customers. We share with our partner what we have learned from the experience and how we will prevent it in the future. That's what they want to see – continuous improvement and a proactive approach.

My clients have lost a lot through this process – sleep, money, employees and peace of mind – they don't need to lose their dignity, too. Neither do you. Stand on your feet. You have something to offer Amazon, and you can salvage this situation.

REINSTATEMENT

Here we are at the end of the book, and some of you are realizing I am not going to write a typical Step-by-Step(SM) on how to write a reinstatement letter. This is because there is no one right answer. There is no perfect phrasing. There is no exact way that you should handle a "New Sold as Used," for example. Our Plans are all customized. I can share my approach, but I have no magic words.

What we realized early on is that there is usually a fundamental underlying reason why our client is suspended – something systemic and endemic in their organization. The suspension is the side-effect of this reason: the natural conclusion. If we are going to fix the problem for them, we have to unearth that reason. To get even more granular, somewhere there is a problem with our client's thinking. It starts there – a thought, an approach – and goes outward to become actions that lead to suspension.

That is what needs to be addressed first. When we explain to Amazon how things are now going to be different, it needs to be *real*. It has to show that the owner's mind has shifted, and with it the entire organization.

And this is not just good intentions. ("I promise to never do it again!") This is backed by action. I had one client who boasted in his first appeal to Amazon how much his customer service team had improved and how well they were treating the customer now. I did an intervention with him and showed him it wasn't true – not even close. I brought out the data, where I showed him actual customer quotes, negative feedback and return reasons. He was stunned, furious and embarrassed. I knew without a doubt that at that moment he changed. He discarded the fantasy and got with the reality. I felt sorry for his customer-service team because someone had lied to the boss, and then he told that lie to Amazon. With me, however, he said "What do we need to do to fix this?"

His Plan was easy to write from there because his Plan was growing by the second as we spoke. He began implementation immediately. He understood *his* mistakes that allowed it to happen. He owned the problem and came up with a solution that worked for him. He has been committed to change ever since, and he reviews his reports every week with his team so they can all be better.

Another client with the same set of performance issues may have a completely different way that he got there. Thus, his Plan is different. If you are suspended and planning to write your own appeal, I strongly suggest you get help from a friend, fellow seller or trusted advisor who will help make sure you have discarded the fantasy of your innocence. Talk through with him/her all the steps that led to the various points of the suspension and what you will do to make sure those problems *can't* happen again.

You also need to look deeply into your account and understand exactly what happened and where the complaints originated. "Not as Described" can be anything from a confusing or misleading listing, to products damaged in shipping, to late products, to the fact that you sent the wrong product. Once you have a clear understanding (and can explain it to Amazon in your Plan), then you can create an appropriate solution to prevent the problems in the future.

I've seen a lot of crazy misinformation on Facebook groups about Plans of Action/appeals, and I'd like to dispel one myth that most of my clients seem to have read. The myth says that your Plan needs to be in bullets and really short because the minions don't want to read long Plans.

Maybe the minions don't want to read long Plans, I don't know, but they certainly read my Plans, and they are often long. The length isn't what is relevant. The thoroughness of the response is. They want to see that you:

- Identified the problem accurately and found out what was really going on.
- Fixed today's issue with the customers and Amazon.
- Created a real Plan with steps and processes to make sure it doesn't happen again.

You need to do this for each ASIN and violation/performance issue they give you. They are supposed to match – the ASINs reflect the issue – but sometimes they don't, so we have to dig deeper. We often find more than one additional ASIN that matches a particular issue, and we put it in the Plan so Amazon can see that we really researched the issue. There's also a good chance that ASIN is on the checklist that you can't see. If you don't include it, they may not reinstate you, or they may make you go back and keep working on the Plan.

We sometimes find other issues that Amazon didn't list in the suspension. Experience has taught us that we should address these in the Plan anyway or else Amazon will just come back and ask for an explanation later. We are trying to save time, because Amazon usually takes so long to respond to its sellers.

Our Plans are succinct. We keep our explanations brief and clear. But they are also thorough. If there are a lot of ASINs or a lot of violations, a Plan can be lengthy. One Plan was 12 pages, single-spaced. That's what it took to cover the 12 performance issues, policy violations and many ASINs the seller had on his suspension notice. He was reinstated in a day.

Plans need to show process. Amazon loves process and understands process. Process is something that can be explained, written down, shared and put in a checklist. Process is something that can reduce errors. In most cases with my clients, their processes (or lack thereof) benefitted from examination.

Take the issue of sending a customer the wrong product, for example. Everyone has done it at some point, I'm sure. For a smaller seller like me, it is often a reflection of being in a hurry, throwing things into boxes before UPS comes to pick up my shipment to Amazon and not taking the time to compare the labels. Sometimes if I had helpers, they would get confused because the abbreviated name on the FNSKU label was similar or the same as another product I was selling. I would know "This is the red one, this is the blue," but they wouldn't.

It is the same with a larger seller; of course, they just have more people to make the mistakes bigger. One of my clients had to recall products several times a year when the CD and the vinyl versions of the album's labels were switched, or the Blue-Ray and the DVD versions of the movie were accidentally switched. By carefully examining this problem, his team realized that they should separate similar items during processing and do them at separate times. That way there aren't piles of the easily confused items in the same shipment or ready to prep at the same time. If the only labels are for the vinyl, you can't sticker the CD by mistake.

There were other processes that this client improved and codified to fix the problem, and I learned a lot. Their solution is not for everyone. Some of my clients don't label their own products before sending them to Amazon. They pay Amazon to label them. Then if there is a problem, it is traced back to Amazon and not my client.

What are your processes that led to the suspension issues? How will you fix them?

Formatting the Plan is also important. If you are filing your first appeal, you will be pasting your Plan into an ugly text box. All your pretty formatting is gone so use what you have – a judicious use of ALL CAPS for section headers or violations, and spacing. Try to make it so someone can scan down your Plan looking for the violations or the ASINs and find them quickly to complete the checklist.

To the best of your ability, make it easy to read. If you have been denied and are submitting a revised Plan, you will be able to paste the Plan into an email which keeps the formatting and spacing better. That helps. If you have invoices, images, charts, etc., you will need to make them into one PDF and link to it. We recommend putting everything into one PDF rather than many attachments.

When writing, use Amazon's language and remember the customers are *their* customers. Try to use the phrase "Amazon's customer" or "the customer" rather than "my customer."

The normal process: appeal. Wait for an answer. If you are not reinstated, they usually have additional questions. Write a revised, second appeal to Seller Performance with answers to their questions. Wait for a response. Repeat until reinstated. They may ask you to add something to the Plan. The "Used sold as New," appeared out of the blue for many of our clients a few weeks ago. Now almost everyone has that claim they have to answer. We rarely saw it before the end of July. By the time you turn in your appeal, there may be another "claim of the month" that you didn't know you'd have to address.

Sellers want to know about writing to Jeff Bezos. They've heard he's the magic bullet that can fix all their problems. We do write letters to Jeff Bezos, but only after we've tried to work with Seller Performance first. Not only is that the correct procedure, but it is hard to write a letter to Jeff asking for his help when we haven't even tried to work with the team he has in place to handle these claims.

It can take weeks to hear back from Bezos' team, so it is not the fastest path to reinstatement either. We look at it as a last resort. It is our "Hail Mary" pass. If the appeal to Jeff fails – which it sometimes does – it is hard to know what to do next. We already went to the boss. If we are going to go back again, we need something new to work with – a compelling reason to submit another Plan and/or a new development.

GET HELP

You don't have to do this all by yourself. It is OK to get help. Having everything rely on you is a recipe for disaster in your business. One bout of the flu and your business could be in trouble, simply because there is no one else to help you. I'm not necessarily talking about hiring a bunch of employees; I'm talking about getting support – from Amazon, other sellers, your family and friends. Have a plan for if you become incapacitated. In business we call it a succession plan. Delegate your areas of weakness. Train your supporters.

I have a team in the Philippines. My assistant Shem has worked with me for years. Although I make my own buying decisions, she can handle almost everything else on my account, from maintenance to customer service to listing errors to reconciliations to research for more inventory. When I go on vacation for a couple of weeks, I don't worry about a thing. Everything's going to be fine. She and her team are affordable and extremely hard-working. I've trained her, and now she's training others.

It is because of this positive experience with Shem and training her for years that I have hired a team to help our clients with ongoing work. We call this "Get Clean Stay Clean." We provide the "Canary Report," which is the weekly warning system for our clients, and we help them clean up their negative feedback, set up Feedback Genius and more. Some of our clients ask us to hire and train a virtual assistant (VA) for their work exclusively. After two months of training, they hire that employee who is now ready to keep their account maintained for them.

Some of our clients who only need part-time support hire us to take care of their needs. They benefit from the fact that there is someone knowledgeable they can call if something isn't working out. We have a trained team of virtual workers and are constantly training new VAs to keep up with the demand.

On the consulting side, we help our clients deal with problems that come up. We help them develop policies and procedures that work for them. We write customer-service letters, remove tricky negative feedback, train their customer-service teams, write answers to policy warnings or closed listing notices, and much more. We have *Seller Hotline* services so they can pick up the phone and call us when they need us, as well as retainer services. We travel to their site, as well as work over the phone.

Each member of our consulting team has more than 20 years of experience working with businesses of all sizes to solve problems. Three of us have also sold on Amazon for more than five years. Our backgrounds bring an understanding to our practice that allows us to quickly get to the bottom of our client's problems.

You don't have to do it all by yourself. We can help. http://onlinesalesstepbystep.com/reinstatement.

REINSTATEMENT NOTES:

- Discard the fantasy of your sales perfection and dive in to the reality.
- Find and fix the underlying systemic and endemic problems – your thoughts, biases, approach and beliefs that are leading to these particular mistakes being made in your organization.
- Be reactive to fix today's problem and proactive to prevent future problems.
- Be specific and show the process.
- Show Amazon you care about the customer by focusing on the customer experience.
- Remember that customers are Amazon's customers.
- Stand on your feet. Own your mistakes and express your sincere regret but don't grovel, don't beg. Be a worthy partner and fix the problem.
- Be succinct – no long-winded explanations or apologies – but thorough.
- Make your Plan easy to read and scan.
- Don't go to Jeff Bezos until you've tried working with Seller Performance.
- Get Help. You don't have to do it alone.

8

Going to the Dark Side

Not all of our clients are reinstated. Some we told up front their chances were slim. Some had failed appeals. The "What do I do now?" question came up. At first, we didn't have a lot we could say. Our focus is on reinstatement and helping sellers comply with Amazon policy. It did not make sense to tell them how to break the rules.

Now, however, I share with them the options we've found online and from talking with other sellers. We don't help them make a decision or encourage them to violate Amazon policy. Our goal is to make it easier for them to get their questions answered, because we will not be able to help them. We had to step over to the dark side to protect ourselves, and we found that it wasn't as hard as we thought.

We have been inside more than 100 suspended and banned accounts since this practice started in February. As sellers ourselves, we were nervous about the idea of our accounts getting linked to theirs. We deal with confidential data with our clients and wanted to keep our communications secure. In addition, we did not want one suspended seller's account to get linked to another because of us. We did not want to be evil cross-pollinating bees, basically.

I read *Amazon Ghost*, which is easily found through a Google search, and I found it very helpful in explaining how Amazon links accounts and people. It allowed us to figure out how to access our clients' accounts safely. We started with the Tor browser (www.torbrowser.com) and Hide My Ass (www.hidemyass.com) to mask our IP addresses, and we moved out from there. We have limited access to our clients' accounts – access that they control – and we have not had any issues to date.

Amazon Ghost teaches sellers how to create a new account and not get caught. I can't verify that everything the author says is true or accurate. I should point out here that while having a second account after you've been banned is against Amazon policy, it is not illegal. You aren't arrested or anything; they just shut down your account (sometimes without an appeal).

One seller I spoke with tried and was caught five times before he was able to keep a new account up for more than a few weeks. There is more than technology involved in setting up a second account. Amazon has its fingers into your personal relationships, bank accounts, credit cards and purchase history. Amazon uses other (highly proprietary) methods to link accounts. This seller has cracked the code for himself and now has multiple accounts.

Another seller chose to buy a corporation. That corporation had a clean, established Amazon account with positive feedback and good metrics. Its owner wanted to retire. While it is not permitted (or legal) to buy and sell an Amazon account, you can buy a business with all its assets, which usually includes inventory, property, logos, names, bank accounts and more. There is no dollar value placed on the account. You are not buying the account. You just happen to own the corporate login, bank account, inventory and credit card now. Amazon's searchbots cannot access public records, so they don't track sales of businesses.

Naturally the new owner needed to be careful to make sure his failed account did not get linked with this new account by not logging in from his old IP address or anything foolish like that. He got a virtual private network (see Hide My Ass above) and a new computer, and is now back in business.

We concluded from our own research that setting up a new account is possible with work and persistence if a client wants to do that.

Some people are heartbroken. They don't want to sell on Amazon anymore. They can still sell off their inventory on eBay and use Amazon to fulfill their eBay or other website orders. This is a good solution for folks who don't want to pay to have their inventory returned to them. They can leave it there and sell it elsewhere. They just need to convert their inventory to multi-channel fulfillment before the 90 days is up or Amazon will destroy it and charge them for it.

Other sellers sell their inventory to another seller and get out of the business altogether.

I hope that no one reading this book will ever need to consider these options. With the information in this book and a commitment to staying clean with Amazon, most sellers should be able to stay on the platform.

While it may take weeks to months, our experience has shown us that most sellers can get reinstated.

Conclusion

The *New York Times* story about how Amazon treats its white collar employees came out just as I was sending this to layout and design. It was shocking and hundreds of news stories and talk shows were spawned from it in just a few days. Facebook combusted. I felt a huge sense of relief. "Maybe they'll believe me after all," I thought.

Much of what I've had to say to my clients and what I've written here is unpopular. "It can't really be that way!" says the mind in denial. "It's not logical!" Unfortunately, it is very, very logical and deeply impersonal.

Birdie Nash was happy. She was back to work after weeks of being suspended from selling. She had learned a lot and was going to make sure she was never suspended again. As she logged in to SellerCentral, she blinked her eyes. Again and again. It couldn't be true! What could she have done in one day to get banned for life!? All the money she lost, all the time she spent writing and re-writing her plan, and then she's reinstated for only one day? Birdie burst into tears.

She didn't know it, but she was a victim of the 18-day glitch. This happened to a number of our clients who were reinstated in less than the 17-day timeframe that Amazon gives you to appeal. For some reason, their reinstatement was not registering...somewhere...and they were getting the form letter that is sent when a seller does not submit a plan – on day 18. Her account was suspended again for no reason. Besides the awful shock, the real shame in this story is that it took nearly a week for Amazon to fix the problem and reinstate her...again.

Tonight a client emailed me with a note from Amazon. Our Jeff Bezos letter had finally worked...sort of. My client had been suspended, reinstated and then suspended again a few days later with the 18-day glitch. We wrote a Jeff letter vociferously requesting the glitch be fixed and my client be reinstated...again. It was insult to injury to make him wait longer. They took nearly two weeks to get back to him.

Jeff Bezos' assistant explained that the reinstatement had been the mistake – not the suspension. This was untrue. The letter suspending my client the second time was definitely the 18-day letter. Next, my client's account was still under review and could he please answer questions about (reasons here). He was reminded that Amazon needed a proactive Plan of Action, not just an explanation of what happened with the ASINs. I thought, "Am I hallucinating, here?" Our Plan – that was obviously still not read – had already addressed those exact reasons and had included a proactive Plan to avoid similar issues from happening again.

My client asked me, "What do we do?" Great question. Since beating my head against a wall is counterproductive, I'll re-write the Plan. This is what it is like to deal with Amazon once you are suspended. No one talks to you, reads your Plan or helps in any way. You are fed misinformation and made to wait a long time if it suits Amazon. When you do reach someone, you are starting again at the bottom like all your work never happened. "Purposeful Darwinism" is really horrible if you are at the bottom.

Amazon's suspension and Plan review system is hugely unfair. Our clients jump through all kinds of hoops in the hopes that they will finally reach a person at Amazon who will look at their Plan and reinstate them. It is shameful and unnecessary. The collective anger of my team on behalf of our clients motivates us. Amazon's actions are not justified. A notice that the rules have changed and that Amazon has raised its standards would be enough for a large portion of their third-party sellers to self-correct behavior that is no longer acceptable. It is the least they can do for their partners.

Because I can only learn by observation and experience (Darwin again), some of my conclusions may prove to be faulty, but this is what I believe today:

- Amazon is purposefully culling its third-party seller herd just as surely as it culls its own workforce...whether they need it or not.
- It is survival of the fittest. These Plans and the waiting game are all about fighting for your right to stay on the platform. They assume a certain percentage

will give up during the process and they'll ban a certain percentage of the rest.

- Persistence is what wins the day more than being right.
- Amazon is using the suspension process to move sellers in a certain direction towards wholesale and private label and away from retail arbitrage, online arbitrage, liquidators and drop shippers.
- The suspensions are Amazon's unofficial announcement that it has raised its standards for its third-party seller.
- Amazon doesn't care that innocent fish are being caught in the nets designed for bigger targets.
- It doesn't matter how long you've sold on the platform, how much money you make them every year, how perfect your metrics are/were.
- Amazon is data and metric driven to an insane level that rips away the humanity and trust that has traditionally been a fundamental underpinning of business. Don't count on your biggest selling partner to be looking out for you.
- Their own employees are encouraged to turn each other in – why on earth would they care about dirty seller tricks or how this suspension might be affecting you? That's life. That's why I have to get my clients reinstated first and then go after the evil sellers. Amazon doesn't care.

One of my editors said to me, "You have convinced me that I will never in a million years be a third-party seller on Amazon. I don't have the patience to play this kind of game or work with a company that cares so little about its relationships." I realize some of you reading this book may feel the same way and I can't blame you. The Amazon today is vastly different from the company I started working with five years ago. It is harder. It is tougher. The message to those selling less than $12 million a year is, "Go away."

Innocent mistakes that I made when I was starting out can get you suspended today like putting the wrong label on a product or accidentally thinking something was a Book but it was actually listed in Toys (and thus you could not sell it as Used). That happened to one of my reinstatement clients *today*. I got a friendly warning when I made mistakes in the past. Today I'd get suspended.

For the rest of you – the ones who think the reward is worth the aggravation and who will be damned if you let Amazon throw you off the platform – I hope this book helps you fight the good fight. Don't give up. Don't take no for an answer. You may have to change some aspects of how you do business, but there is still a lot of money to be made.

Amazon is one of the greatest wealth platforms ever created. You deserve your piece of it. You are now forewarned and forearmed. Go forth and conquer.

Glossary

Amazonians – People who work for Amazon. They call themselves that.

ASIN – Amazon Standard Identification Number. Amazon assigns a unique ASIN to every product and product variation in its catalog. It is unique to a *page* on Amazon versus a particular product on Amazon. Pronounced "A-SIN," an ASIN is how Amazon usually identifies problems to you in performance notifications. This ties the problem directly to *your* listing on that particular Amazon page. This is particularly important if you sell many versions/colors/variations of a product.

Banned – This is where you have exhausted your appeals and Amazon tells you not to write them back any more. Your letter tells you that your funds will be released in 90 days and that to open a new account would be a violation of Amazon policy. From Amazon's perspective, you are gone and they are done with you. Getting their attention at this point is difficult and can take a long time.

Buy Box – This is the price a customer sees on Amazon.com when they got to a product's main page. Generally there are several offers that rotate through the Buy Box – all within a few percentage points of each other. While FBA sellers get priority over MF, the negative feedback rate can also affect how much time (if any) your offer gets in the Buy Box. Since more than 70% of sales on Amazon are made from the Buy Box, it is important to give yourself every advantage to maximize your time there.

Case Log – Part of Seller Central, the case log is for routine correspondence between you and Amazon. This is where cases are resolved like, "Am I approved in grocery?" or where you find the results of negative feedback removal requests. Serious correspondence requiring your attention will be found under "performance notifications."

The Checklist – I'm not sure if there really is a suspension checklist but it seems likely that there is one based on observation. If your plan doesn't hit on all the topics about you in Amazon's files, they won't reinstate you. We've been lucky a few times to have an Amazonian pull up the problems in our clients' accounts for us and let us know what we had to address to get them reinstated.

Commingled Inventory – A couple of years ago, I called commingling an Amazon social disease. I had no idea how right I was. Whether or not you choose commingling, your New FBA inventory can be commingled when Amazon is in a hurry to ship something out. The problem arises when another seller has mixed faulty, shoddy, ugly (dinged-up) product in with your pristine units. Sellers who use commingling benefit from fewer expenses (no need for FNSKU labels, for example) and can ship directly to Amazon's warehouse from their suppliers. Because their units are not labeled, however, they are on the hook for other sellers' mistakes. That customer complaint about your product? They may not have even gotten your unit – but you can't prove it. My clients strongly resist it due to added expense, but I encourage all sellers to have their items FNSKU-labeled even when deliberately commingling. It protects them from future problems if they can take a picture of the barcode and say to Amazon, "That's not my FNSKU on the package." Think of an FNSKU label as your inventory condom.

Denied – If your original appeal is denied, you usually can still submit a revised Plan of Action. While they won't review it as quickly as they reviewed your original appeal, there is still a good chance you can be reinstated.

Drop shipping – This practice, while not disallowed by Amazon, is strongly discouraged. One of the clearest ways they discourage this practice is by suspending sellers who show certain characteristics common to drop shippers: late shipments, incorrect orders, seller-cancelled orders, faulty products and more. I can often tell if a seller is drop shipping just by looking at the problems in his/her account. Drop shipping from another online retailer *is* forbidden. Your receipts will be useless if they show you were drop shipping product to Amazon's customers from an online retailer.

FBA – Fulfillment by Amazon. This is Amazon's program through which sellers send inventory to Amazon for fulfillment. The key feature of this program as it relates to getting suspended is that Amazon generally takes responsibility for all fulfillment issues and doesn't hold them against the seller. My FBA clients are rarely suspended for performance issues. Instead, they are suspended mostly for policy violations. I have some clients who sell both MF and FBA. They are still vulnerable to performance metric suspensions for their MF sales.

FNSKU – Amazon's Fulfillment Network SKU identifier. This is your unique product identifier to Amazon. It tells Amazon's warehouse workers everything about that item – your name, SKU, how many units there are; the condition; the day it arrived…everything. With FBA inventory, this number and barcode is placed over the UPC barcode of the product. Merchants don't need to have an FNSKU because they fulfill their own inventory.

Liquidators – Amazon frowns on this source of inventory. Generally, liquidators buy goods by the truck-load from retailers and other commercial enterprises and re-sell them "as is." The opportunity for a seller is to buy potentially quality merchandise for a low price. The problem is that there are often returns and faulty products mixed in with the good. There can be counterfeit goods, expired items and much more. Amazon can't stop you from buying from liquidators, but when they suspend you, they won't accept invoices/receipts from liquidators as legitimate. This is a huge problem if you are suspended for "counterfeit." Bought from some dealer on eBay or Craigslist? You are in a pickle. Experienced sellers of liquidation merchandise have teams of inventory checkers that weed out the repackages and returns from the New and who test all the electronics products (which have to be sold as "Like-New" instead of "New"). Even so, these sellers are highly vulnerable to claims of counterfeit. Buying from liquidators is risky behavior for most sellers from a suspension perspective.

MAP – Minimum Advertised Price. This usually refers to an agreed-upon price below which an authorized reseller will not sell a manufacturer's product. It is not considered price-fixing by the industry or Amazon. If you have an agreement with a manufacturer and "break MAP," they will not sell to you again (generally), unless you are Amazon, apparently. Amazon breaks MAP all the time and still has plenty of product to sell. The manufacturer might also tell Amazon that you are no longer authorized to sell their product. This is a hotly contested issue because, as I mentioned, Amazon breaks MAP all the time. If you can't lower your price to compete with them, what is the point of selling that product?

Merchant Fulfilled – This is where the seller fulfills his/her own orders. Sellers will often choose to fulfill their own orders because they can do it less expensively than sending it to Amazon...or that is their perception. They may also be selling items that are so large that Amazon's FBA fees would be impractical. Some merchants are selling inventory they don't actually own (drop shipping), so they have to quickly purchase and arrange to deliver merchandise once they sell an item.

Messages – This is where Amazon keeps correspondence between you and your customers. If you sell FBA, Amazon will handle a lot of customer service, returns, etc., for you. *However,* be aware that if the customer reaches out to you for any reason, you are responsible for handling the correspondence. Even if the answer is to send them back to Amazon, you must respond in less than 24 hours. This includes weekends and holidays.

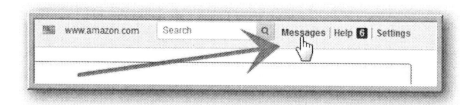

Minions – Also known as worker bees, employees, workers. I use the term to specifically describe a task-oriented person who is working from a template/checklist rather than problem-solving or analyzing.

ODR – Order Defect Rate. Amazon sets the desirable ODR rate at 1% or less. This is a performance metric that includes negative feedback, A-to-Z claims, returns and imperfect orders. The rate by itself is not the whole story, however. You can have an ODR of less than 1% and still be suspended if any single ASIN is making up too much of that rate.

Performance Notification – Amazon notifies you of problems in your account through performance notifications. You will find these in Seller Central under "Performance" at the top of the page.

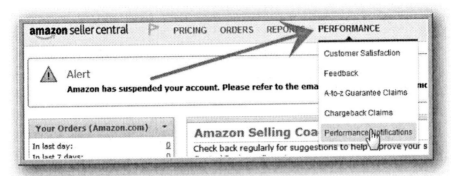

You should also get an email every time Amazon posts a new performance notification. If you use the Amazon Seller App on your phone, you can arrange your settings to get a notification on your phone every time you have a performance notice (works for customer messages as well). This is where Amazon puts suspension notices (*not the case log*) and where you file your appeal.

Performance Metric Violation – Amazon holds a high standard of performance for itself and its sellers. When you fall below its required metrics, you will usually receive a warning and then be suspended. Some performance issues like negative feedback rate can be fixed pretty quickly. Others are measured over time and take weeks to months to improve.

Plan of Action – Every time a seller loses the right to sell on an ASIN or has his account suspended, Amazon requests a Plan of Action detailing how the seller is going to fix the problem so it doesn't happen again. Simply saying "I won't do it again" is not enough.

Policy Violation – Amazon has an ever-growing list of what constitutes policy violations. Selling counterfeit products, copyright infringement and selling forbidden products are just a few examples of Amazon's rules. A complete list can be found on Seller Central "Help."

Searchbot – The word I use to describe the automated keyword-search, algorithm-based process that gets sellers suspended. I also use "Robot."

Seller Central – All Amazon sellers conduct business on the Amazon platform through "Seller Central." You find it by logging in at: http://sellercentral.amazon.com for the US platform (or ".co.uk" for the UK or ".de" for Germany, or ".ca" for Canada – you get the idea). This is the repository for *all* communications and information about selling on Amazon. If you have a question, it is most likely addressed in a report or through Seller Central "Help."

Suspended – Amazon has shut down all your listings and is holding on to your money. You are given 17 days to appeal their decision. They want to see a Plan of Action before they consider reinstating you. If you are suspended, many activities on your account are shut down, including access to Seller Support, automated negative feedback removal and more.

SKU – Stock Keeping Unit. This is the unique identifier for a product, usually but not always represented as a number and barcode. Often the manufacturer's SKU for an item is the UPC or ISBN#. The seller's SKU for the same item is called an MSKU ("merchant stock keeping unit"). Amazon's unique identifier for inventory fulfilled by Amazon is called the FNSKU.

Appendix I: Amazon Prohibited Seller Activities and Actions

As of August 25, 2015

These Prohibited Seller Activities and Actions are established to maintain a selling platform that is safe for buyers and fair for sellers of both products and services. Failure to comply with the terms of this policy can result in cancellation of listings, suspension from use of Amazon.com tools and reports, and/or the removal of selling privileges.

Note: This policy is in addition to, and in no way limits, your other obligations pursuant to your seller agreement or otherwise.

GENERAL GUIDELINES

The following guidelines apply to both sellers of products and services. For guidelines specific to products or services, see the information following this section.

- **Attempts to divert transactions or buyers:** Any attempt to circumvent the established Amazon.com sales process or to divert Amazon.com users to another website or sales process is prohibited. Specifically, any advertisements, marketing messages (special offers) or "calls to action" that lead, prompt, or encourage Amazon.com users to leave the Amazon.com website are prohibited. Prohibited activities include the following:

- The use of email intended to divert customers away from the Amazon.com sales process.
- The inclusion of hyperlinks, URLs or web addresses within any seller generated confirmation email messages or any product/listing description fields that are intended to divert customers away from the Amazon.com sales process.

- **Unauthorized & improper business names:** The Business Name (identifying a seller's business entity on Amazon.com) must be a name that: accurately identifies the seller; is not misleading; and the seller has the right to use (that is, the name cannot include the trademark of, or otherwise infringe on, any trademark or other intellectual property right of any person). Furthermore, a seller cannot use a business name that contains an email suffix such as .com, .net, .biz, and so on.

- **Inappropriate email communications:** All email communications with buyers must be courteous, relevant and appropriate. Unsolicited email communications with Amazon.com users, email communications other than as necessary for order fulfillment and related customer service, and emails containing marketing communications of any kind (including within otherwise permitted communications) are prohibited.

- **Direct email addresses:** Buyers and sellers may communicate with one another via the Buyer-Seller Messaging Service, which assigns unique Amazon-generated email addresses to both parties. Sellers are prohibited from providing or soliciting direct, non-Amazon-generated email addresses on the Amazon.com website or in correspondence through the Buyer-Seller Messaging Service.

- **Operating multiple seller accounts:** Operating and maintaining multiple Seller Central accounts is prohibited. If you have a legitimate business need for a second account, you can apply for an exception to this policy. From the bottom of any page in your seller account, click Contact Seller Support. Select **Your account**, then select **Other account issues**.

In your request, provide an explanation of the legitimate business need for a second account. To be considered for approval, you must have the following:

1. An account in good standing with excellent Customer Metrics
2. A separate email address and bank account for the new account
3. No intention to sell the same products or services in both accounts
4. Intention to sell in entirely different categories
5. The inventory sold in each account must be different

You'll receive a response to your request within 2 to 3 business days.

- **Misuse of the Amazon selling platform:** All sellers are able to access and use the Amazon.com selling platform. If a seller uploads excessive amounts of data repeatedly, or otherwise uses the platform in an excessive or unreasonable way, it can create a disproportional load on the platform and impair the ability of other sellers to easily access and use the platform. If a seller is misusing or making excessive or unreasonable use of the Amazon.com selling platform, Amazon may in its sole discretion restrict or block the seller's access to product feeds or any other platform functions that are being misused until the seller stops its misuse.
- **Misuse of ratings, feedback, or reviews:** Any attempt to manipulate ratings, feedback, or reviews is prohibited.
  - Ratings and feedback: The rating and feedback features allow buyers to evaluate the overall performance of a seller, helping sellers to develop a reputation within the Amazon Marketplace. You may not post abusive or inappropriate feedback or include personal information about a transaction partner. This also includes posting ratings or feedback to your own account. You may request feedback from a buyer, however you may not pay or offer any incentive to a buyer for either providing or removing feedback.
  - Reviews: Reviews are important to the Amazon Marketplace, providing a forum for feedback about product and service details and reviewers' experiences with products and services — positive or negative. You may not write reviews for products or services that you have a financial interest in, including reviews for products or services that you or your competitors sell. Additionally, you may not

provide compensation for a review other than a free copy of the product. If you offer a free product, it must be clear that you are soliciting an **unbiased** review. The free product must be provided in advance. No refunds are permitted after the review is written. You may not intentionally manipulate your products' rankings, including by offering an excessive number of free or discounted products, in exchange for a review. Review solicitations that ask for only positive reviews or that offer compensation are prohibited. You may not ask buyers to remove negative reviews.

- **Misuse of sales rank:** The best seller rank feature allows buyers to evaluate the popularity of a product. You may not solicit or knowingly accept fake or fraudulent orders. This includes placing orders for your own products. You may not provide compensation to buyers for purchasing your products or provide claim codes to buyers for the purpose of inflating sales rank. In addition, you may not make claims regarding a product's best seller rank in the product detail page information, including the title and description.

- **Misuse of the Amazon.com A-to-z Guarantee:** Any misuse of the Amazon.com A-to-z Guarantee claims process is prohibited. Sellers who have an excessive number or dollar amount of A-to-z Guarantee claims are subject to termination. In cases where a buyer is dissatisfied with a product or service, buyers can contact the seller to make arrangements for a refund, return, or exchange, as appropriate. Amazon reserves the right to seek reimbursement from the seller if we reimburse a buyer under the terms of the Amazon.com A-to-z Guarantee.

ADDITIONAL GUIDELINES FOR SELLERS

The following guidelines apply to sellers of products:

- **Shipment of BMVD Products :** Books, Music, Video, and DVD products offered through Amazon.com must be shipped within two business days of the date the order confirmation is made available to you.

- **Post-transaction price manipulation and excessive shipping fees:** Any attempt to increase the sale price of an item after a transaction has been completed is prohibited. Additionally, sellers cannot set excessive order fulfillment and shipping costs.

- **Matching product offerings inaccurately:** When listing items for sale using an existing product detail page, the product being offered must be listed on a product detail page that accurately describes the product in all respects, including with respect to the following attributes: manufacturer, edition, binding, version, format, or player compatibility. Sellers may not match their item to a detail page with a different ISBN, UPC, EAN, or other external identifier.

  Exception: Club editions of audio CDs should be listed against the detail page for the standard edition of the CD, even if the UPCs of the two editions are different, if the following criteria are met:
  - The content on both editions is identical; and
  - A page with the UPC for the club edition does not already exist in our catalog. Use the listing comments to indicate that the item is a club edition. Format of the products (CD) must be identical.

- **Creating duplicate product detail pages:** Creating a product detail page for a product already in the Amazon.com catalog is prohibited.

- **Creating separate listings:** Sellers may not create separate listings for identical copies of the same item. Individually listing the same item several times is confusing for buyers and frustrating for other sellers. Sellers must use the quantity field to offer multiple copies of the same item, and only list separately if offering the same item in different conditions.

- Pre-sells of BMVD Products: Sellers should not list or match against Books, Music, Video, or DVD products that Amazon designates as pre-orderable. BMVD Products offered through Amazon.com must be shipped within two business days of the date the order confirmation is made available to you. It is also important to maintain accurate inventory records, as instances of "stock-outs" could be reflected in your seller feedback rating. If an item you are offering will not be available for immediate shipping upon order, either cancel the order or alert the buyer, and initiate a refund if necessary. Amazon will immediately cancel any seller listing for Books, Music, Video or DVD items that Amazon designates as pre-orderable.

ADDITIONAL GUIDELINES FOR SERVICE PROVIDERS

The following guidelines apply to service providers:

- **Upselling:** The service provider must perform the service as outlined in the scope of work on the service detail page on the date the service was purchased. The service provider may not solicit additional product, parts or service orders before, during or after the service call.

  If the buyer requests services, parts, or products outside of the defined scope of work, then the service provider may fulfill that request and charge the buyer directly.

- **Unapproved technicians:** For in-home services, if you send a non-approved technician to fulfill a service order, your selling privileges may be removed

Appendix II: Your Contract with Amazon

As of August 25, 2015

GENERAL TERMS

Welcome to **Amazon Services Business Solutions**, a suite of optional services for sellers including: Selling on Amazon, Amazon Webstore, Fulfillment by Amazon, Amazon Clicks, and Transaction Processing Services.

THIS AMAZON SERVICES BUSINESS SOLUTIONS AGREEMENT (THE **"AGREEMENT"**) CONTAINS THE TERMS AND CONDITIONS THAT GOVERN YOUR ACCESS TO AND USE OF THE SERVICES AND IS AN AGREEMENT BETWEEN YOU OR THE BUSINESS YOU REPRESENT AND AMAZON. BY REGISTERING FOR OR USING THE SERVICES, YOU (ON BEHALF OF YOURSELF OR THE BUSINESS YOU REPRESENT) AGREE TO BE BOUND BY THE TERMS OF THIS AGREEMENT, INCLUDING THE SERVICE TERMS AND PROGRAM POLICIES THAT APPLY FOR EACH COUNTRY FOR WHICH YOU REGISTER OR ELECT TO USE A SERVICE (IN EACH CASE, THE "ELECTED COUNTRY").

As used in this Agreement, **"we," "us,"** and **"Amazon"** means the applicable Amazon Contracting Party and any of its applicable Affiliates, and **"you"** means the applicant (if registering for or using a Service as an individual), or the business employing the applicant (if registering for or using a Service as a business) and any of its Affiliates. Capitalized terms have the meanings given to them in this Agreement. If there is a conflict among terms in this Agreement, the Program Policies will prevail over any applicable Service Terms and the General Terms, and the applicable Service Terms will prevail over the General Terms.

1. Enrollment.

To begin the enrollment process, you must complete the registration process for one or more of the Services. Use of the Services is limited to parties that can lawfully enter into and form contracts under applicable law (for example, the Elected Country may not allow minors to use the Services). As part of the application, you must provide us with your (or your business') legal name, address, phone number and e-mail address. We may at any time cease providing any or all of the Services at our sole discretion and without notice.

2. Service Fee Payments; Receipt of Sales Proceeds.

Fee details are described in the applicable Service Terms and Program Policies. You are responsible for all of your expenses in connection with this Agreement. To use a Service, you must provide us with valid credit card information from a credit card or credit cards acceptable by Amazon (**"Your Credit Card"**) as well as valid bank account information for a bank account or bank accounts acceptable by Amazon (conditions for acceptance may be modified or discontinued by us at any time without notice) (**"Your Bank Account"**). You will use only a name you are authorized to use in connection with a Service and will update all of the information you provide to us in connection with the Services as necessary to ensure that it at all times remains accurate, complete and valid. You authorize us (and will provide us documentation evidencing your authorization upon our request) to verify your information (including any updated information), to obtain credit reports about you from time to time, to obtain credit authorizations from the issuer of Your Credit Card, and to charge Your Credit Card or debit Your Bank Account for any sums payable by you to us (in reimbursement or otherwise). All payments to you will be remitted to Your Bank Account through a banking network or by other means specified by us.

For any amounts you owe us, we may (a) charge Your Credit Card or any other payment instrument you provide to us; (b) offset any amounts that are payable by you to us (in reimbursement or otherwise) against any payments we may make to you; (c) invoice you for amounts due to us, in which case you will pay the invoiced amounts upon receipt; (d) reverse any credits to Your Bank Account; or (e) collect payment or reimbursement from you by any other lawful means. Except as provided otherwise, all amounts contemplated in this Agreement will be expressed and displayed in the

Local Currency, and all payments contemplated by this Agreement will be made in the Local Currency. If we discover erroneous or duplicate transactions, then we reserve the right to seek reimbursement from you by deducting from future payments owed to you, charging Your Credit Card, or seeking such reimbursement from you by any other lawful means.

IF WE DETERMINE THAT YOUR ACTIONS OR PERFORMANCE MAY RESULT IN RETURNS, CHARGEBACKS, CLAIMS, DISPUTES, OR OTHER RISKS, THEN WE MAY IN OUR SOLE DISCRETION WITHHOLD ANY PAYMENTS TO YOU UNTIL THE COMPLETION OF ANY RELATED INVESTIGATION. IF WE DETERMINE THAT YOUR ACCOUNT HAS BEEN USED TO ENGAGE IN DECEPTIVE, FRAUDULENT, OR ILLEGAL ACTIVITY, THEN WE MAY IN OUR SOLE DISCRETION PERMANENTLY WITHHOLD ANY PAYMENTS.

As a security measure, we may, but are not required to, impose transaction limits on some or all customers and sellers relating to the value of any transaction or disbursement, the cumulative value of all transactions or disbursements during a period of time, or the number of transactions per day or other period of time. We will not be liable to you: (i) if we do not proceed with a transaction or disbursement that would exceed any limit established by us for a security reason, or (ii) if we permit a customer to withdraw from a transaction because an Amazon Site or Service is unavailable following the commencement of a transaction.

3. Term and Termination.

The term of this Agreement will start on the date of your completed registration for or use of a Service, whichever occurs first, and continue until terminated by us or you as provided in this Agreement (the **"Term"**). We may terminate or suspend this Agreement or any Service for any reason at any time by notice to you. You may terminate this Agreement or any Service or the Promotion Site for any reason at any time by the means then specified by Amazon. Termination or suspension of a Service will not terminate or suspend any other Service unless explicitly provided. Upon termination, all rights and obligations of the parties under this Agreement will terminate, except that Sections 2, 3, 4, 5, 6, 7, 8, 9, 11, 14, 15, 16 and 18 will survive termination. Any terms that expressly survive according to the applicable Service Terms will also survive termination.

4. License.

You grant us a royalty-free, non-exclusive, worldwide, perpetual, irrevocable right and license to use, reproduce, perform, display, distribute, adapt, modify, re-format, create derivative works of, and otherwise commercially or non-commercially exploit in any manner, any and all of Your Materials, and to sublicense the foregoing rights to our Affiliates and operators of Amazon Associated Properties; provided, however, that we will not alter any of Your Trademarks from the form provided by you (except to re-size trademarks to the extent necessary for presentation, so long as the relative proportions of such trademarks remain the same) and will comply with your removal requests as to specific uses of Your Trademarks (provided you are unable to do so using standard functionality made available to you via the applicable Amazon Site or Service); provided further, however, that nothing in this Agreement will prevent or impair our right to use Your Materials without your consent to the extent that such use is allowable without a license from you or your Affiliates under applicable law (e.g., fair use under United States copyright law, referential use under trademark law, or valid license from a third party).

5. Representations.

You represent and warrant to us that: (a) if you are a business, you are duly organized, validly existing and in good standing under the Laws of the country in which your business is registered and that you are registering for the Service(s) within such country; (b) you have all requisite right, power and authority to enter into this Agreement, perform your obligations, and grant the rights, licenses and authorizations in this Agreement; (c) any information provided or made available by you or your Affiliates to Amazon or its Affiliates is at all times accurate and complete; and (d) you and all of your subcontractors, agents and suppliers will comply with all applicable Laws in your performance of your obligations and exercise of your rights under this Agreement.

6. Indemnification.

You release us and agree to indemnify, defend and hold harmless us, our Affiliates, and our and their respective officers, directors, employees, representatives and agents against any claim, loss, damage, settlement, cost, expense or other liability (including, without limitation, attorneys' fees) (each, a "Claim") arising from or related to: (a) your actual or alleged breach of any obligations in this Agreement; (b) any of Your Sales Channels other than Amazon Sites and Amazon Associated Properties, Your Products (including their offer, sale, performance and fulfillment), Your Materials, any actual or alleged infringement of any Intellectual Property Rights by any of the foregoing, and any personal injury, death or property damage related thereto; (c) Your Personnel (including any act or omission of Your Personnel or any Claim brought or directed by Your Personnel); or (d) Your Taxes. You will use counsel reasonably satisfactory to us to defend each indemnified Claim. If at any time we reasonably determine that any indemnified Claim might adversely affect us, we may take control of the defense at our expense. You may not consent to the entry of any judgment or enter into any settlement of a Claim without our prior written consent, which may not be unreasonably withheld.

7. Disclaimer & General Release.
a. THE AMAZON SITES AND THE SERVICES, INCLUDING ALL CONTENT, SOFTWARE, FUNCTIONS, MATERIALS AND INFORMATION MADE AVAILABLE ON OR PROVIDED IN CONNECTION WITH THE SERVICES, ARE PROVIDED "AS-IS." AS A USER OF THE SERVICES, YOU USE THE AMAZON SITES, THE SERVICES AND SELLER CENTRAL AT YOUR OWN RISK. TO THE FULLEST EXTENT PERMISSIBLE BY LAW, WE AND OUR AFFILIATES DISCLAIM: (i) ANY REPRESENTATIONS OR WARRANTIES REGARDING THIS AGREEMENT, THE SERVICES OR THE TRANSACTIONS CONTEMPLATED BY THIS AGREEMENT, INCLUDING ANY IMPLIED WARRANTIES OF MERCHANTABILITY, FITNESS FOR A PARTICULAR PURPOSE OR NON-INFRINGEMENT; (ii) IMPLIED WARRANTIES ARISING OUT OF COURSE OF DEALING, COURSE OF PERFORMANCE OR USAGE OF TRADE; AND (iii) ANY OBLIGATION, LIABILITY, RIGHT, CLAIM OR REMEDY IN TORT, WHETHER OR NOT ARISING FROM OUR NEGLIGENCE. WE DO NOT WARRANT THAT THE FUNCTIONS CONTAINED IN THE AMAZON SITES AND THE SERVICES WILL MEET YOUR REQUIREMENTS OR BE AVAILABLE, TIMELY, SECURE, UNINTERRUPTED OR ERROR FREE, AND WE WILL NOT BE LIABLE FOR ANY SERVICE INTERRUPTIONS, INCLUDING BUT NOT LIMITED TO SYSTEM FAILURES OR OTHER INTERRUPTIONS THAT MAY AFFECT THE RECEIPT, PROCESSING, ACCEPTANCE, COMPLETION OR SETTLEMENT OF ANY TRANSACTIONS.

b. BECAUSE AMAZON IS NOT INVOLVED IN TRANSACTIONS BETWEEN CUSTOMERS AND SELLERS OR OTHER PARTICIPANT DEALINGS, IF A DISPUTE ARISES BETWEEN ONE OR MORE PARTICIPANTS, EACH PARTICIPANT RELEASES AMAZON (AND ITS AGENTS AND EMPLOYEES) FROM CLAIMS, DEMANDS, AND DAMAGES (ACTUAL AND CONSEQUENTIAL) OF EVERY KIND AND NATURE, KNOWN AND UNKNOWN, SUSPECTED AND UNSUSPECTED, DISCLOSED AND UNDISCLOSED, ARISING OUT OF OR IN ANY WAY CONNECTED WITH SUCH DISPUTES.

8. Limitation of Liability.

WE WILL NOT BE LIABLE (WHETHER IN CONTRACT, WARRANTY, TORT (INCLUDING NEGLIGENCE, PRODUCT LIABILITY OR OTHER THEORY) OR OTHERWISE) TO YOU OR ANY OTHER PERSON FOR COST OF COVER, RECOVERY OR RECOUPMENT OF ANY INVESTMENT MADE BY YOU OR YOUR AFFILIATES IN CONNECTION WITH THIS AGREEMENT, OR FOR ANY LOSS OF PROFIT, REVENUE, BUSINESS, OR DATA OR PUNITIVE OR CONSEQUENTIAL DAMAGES ARISING OUT OF OR RELATING TO THIS AGREEMENT, EVEN IF AMAZON HAS BEEN ADVISED OF THE POSSIBILITY OF THOSE COSTS OR DAMAGES. FURTHER, OUR AGGREGATE LIABILITY ARISING OUT OF OR IN CONNECTION WITH THIS AGREEMENT OR THE TRANSACTIONS CONTEMPLATED WILL NOT EXCEED AT ANY TIME THE TOTAL AMOUNTS DURING THE PRIOR SIX MONTH PERIOD PAID BY YOU TO AMAZON IN CONNECTION WITH THE PARTICULAR SERVICE GIVING RISE TO THE CLAIM.

9. Insurance.

If the gross proceeds from Your Transactions exceed the applicable Insurance Threshold during each month over any period of three (3) consecutive months, or otherwise if requested by us, then within thirty (30) days thereafter, you will maintain at your expense throughout the remainder of the Term for each applicable Elected Country commercial general, umbrella or excess liability insurance with the Insurance Limits per occurrence and in aggregate covering liabilities caused by or occurring in conjunction with the operation of your business, including products, products/com-pleted operations and bodily injury, with policy(ies) naming Amazon and its assignees as additional insureds. At our request, you will provide to us certificates of insurance for the coverage to the following address: c/o Amazon, P.O. Box 81226, Seattle, WA 98108-1226, Attention: Risk Management.

10. Tax Matters.

As between the parties, you will be responsible for the collection, reporting and payment of any and all of Your Taxes, except to the extent Amazon expressly agrees to receive taxes or other transaction-based charges in connection with tax calculation services made available by Amazon and used by you. You agree to and will comply with the Tax Policies. All fees payable by you to Amazon under this Agreement or the applicable Service Terms are exclusive of any applicable taxes, and you will be responsible for paying Amazon any of Your Taxes imposed on such fees.

11. Confidentiality.

During the course of your use of the Services, you may receive information relating to us or to the Services, including but not limited to Amazon Transaction Information, that is not known to the general public ("Confidential Information"). You agree that: (a) all Confidential Information will remain Amazon's exclusive property; (b) you will use Confidential Information only as is reasonably necessary for your participation in the Services; (c) you will not otherwise disclose Confidential Information to any other Person; and (d) you will take all reasonable measures to protect the Confidential Information against any use or disclosure that is not expressly permitted in this Agreement. You may not issue any press release or make any public statement related to the Services, or use our name, trademarks or logo, in any way (including in promotional material) without our advance written permission, or misrepresent or embellish the relationship between us in any way.

12. Force Majeure.

We will not be liable for any delay or failure to perform any of our obligations under this Agreement by reasons, events or other matters beyond our reasonable control.

13. Relationship of Parties.

Subject to the Transaction Processing Service Terms (if the Elected Country for a Service is the United States), you and we are independent contractors, and nothing in this Agreement will create any partnership, joint venture, agency, franchise, sales representative, or employment relationship between us. You will have no authority to make or accept any offers or representations on our behalf. This Agreement will not create an exclusive relationship between you and us. Nothing expressed or mentioned in or implied from this Agreement is intended or will be construed to give to any person other than the parties to this Agreement any legal or equitable right, remedy, or claim under or in respect to this Agreement. This Agreement and all of the representations, warranties, covenants, conditions, and provisions in this Agreement are intended to be and are for the sole and exclusive benefit of Amazon, you, and customers. As between you and us, you will be solely responsible for all obligations associated with the use of any third party service or feature that you permit us to use on your behalf, including compliance with any applicable terms of use. You will not make any statement, whether on your site or otherwise, that would contradict anything in this section.

14. Use of Amazon Transaction Information.

You will not, and will cause your Affiliates not to, directly or indirectly: (a) disclose any Amazon Transaction Information (except that you may disclose that information solely as necessary for you to perform your obligations under this Agreement if you ensure that every recipient uses the information only for that purpose and complies with the restrictions applicable to you related to that information); (b) use any Amazon Transaction Information for any marketing or promotional purposes whatsoever, or otherwise in any way inconsistent with our or your privacy policies or applicable Law; (c) contact a Person that has ordered Your Product with the intent to collect any amounts in connection therewith or to influence that Person to make an alternative transaction; (d) disparage us, our Affiliates, or any of their or our respective products or services or any customer; or (e) target communications of any kind on the basis of the intended recipient being an Amazon Site user. In addition, you may only use tools and methods that we designate to communicate with Amazon Site users regarding Your Transactions, including for the purpose of scheduling, communicating, or cancelling the fulfillment of Your Products. The terms of this Section 14 do not prevent you from using other information that you acquire without reference to Amazon Transaction Information for any purpose, even if that information is identical to Amazon Transaction Information, provided that you do not target communications on the basis of the intended recipient being an Amazon Site user.

15. Suggestions and Other Information.

If you or any of your Affiliates elect to provide or make available suggestions, comments, ideas, improvements, or other feedback or materials to us in connection with or related to any Amazon Site or Service (including any related Technology), we will be free to use, disclose, reproduce, modify, license, transfer and otherwise distribute, and exploit any of the foregoing information or materials in any manner. In order to cooperate with governmental requests, to protect our systems and customers, or to ensure the integrity and operation of our business and systems, we may access and disclose any information we consider necessary or appropriate, including but not limited to user contact details, IP addresses and traffic information, usage history and posted content.

16. Modification.

We may amend any of the terms and conditions contained in this Agreement at any time and at our sole discretion. Any changes will be effective upon the posting of such changes on Seller Central or on the applicable Amazon Site, and you are responsible for reviewing these locations and informing yourself of all applicable changes or notices. All notice of changes to the General Terms and the Service Terms will be posted for at least 30 days. Changes to Program Policies may be made without notice to you. You should refer regularly to Seller Central to review the current Agreement (including the Service Terms and Program Policies) and to be sure that the items you offer can be offered via the applicable Service. YOUR CONTINUED USE OF A SERVICE AFTER AMAZON'S POSTING OF ANY CHANGES WILL CONSTITUTE YOUR ACCEPTANCE OF SUCH CHANGES OR MODIFICATIONS.

17. Password Security.

Any password we provide to you may be used only during the Term to access Seller Central (or other tools we provide) to use the Services, electronically accept Your Transactions, and review your completed transactions. You are solely responsible for maintaining the security of your password. You may not disclose your password to any third party (other than third parties authorized by you to use your account in accordance with this Agreement) and are solely responsible for any use of or action taken under your password. If your password is compromised, you must immediately change your password.

18. Miscellaneous.

The Governing Laws will govern this Agreement, without reference to rules governing choice of laws or the Convention on Contracts for the International Sale of Goods. If the Elected Country is Japan, Amazon and you both consent that any dispute with Amazon or its Affiliates or claim relating in any way to your use of the Services or this Agreement as it relates to your use of the Services in Japan will be adjudicated in the Governing Courts, and you consent to exclusive jurisdiction and venue in the Governing Courts. **If the Elected Country is the United States, Canada, or Mexico, Amazon and you both consent that any dispute with Amazon or its Affiliates or claim relating in any way to this Agreement or your use of the Services will be resolved by binding arbitration as described in this paragraph, rather than in court,** except that (i) you may assert claims in a small claims court that is a Governing Court if your claims qualify and (ii) you or we may bring suit in the Governing Courts, submitting to the jurisdiction of the Governing Courts and waiving our respective rights to any other jurisdiction, to enjoin infringement or other misuse of intellectual property rights. **There is no judge or jury in arbitration, and court review of an arbitration award is limited. However, an arbitrator can award on an individual basis the same damages and relief as a court (including injunctive and declaratory relief or statutory damages), and must follow the terms of this Agreement as a court would.** To begin an arbitration proceeding, you must send a letter requesting arbitration and describing your claim to our registered agent, CSC Services of Nevada, Inc., 2215-B Renaissance Drive, Las Vegas, NV 89119. The arbitration will be conducted by the American Arbitration Association (AAA) under its rules, including the AAA's Supplementary Procedures for Consumer-Related Disputes. Payment of all filing, administration and arbitrator fees will be governed by the AAA's rules. We will reimburse those fees for claims totaling less than $10,000 unless the arbitrator determines the claims are frivolous. Likewise, Amazon will not seek attorneys' fees and costs from you in arbitration unless the arbitrator determines the claims are frivolous. You may choose to have the arbitration conducted by telephone, based on written submissions, or in person in the county where you live or at another mutually agreed location. **Amazon and you each agree that any dispute resolution proceedings will be conducted only on an individual basis and not in a class, consolidated or representative action.** If for any reason a claim proceeds in court rather than in arbitration **Amazon and you each waive any right to a jury trial.**

You may not assign this Agreement, by operation of law or otherwise, without our prior written consent. Subject to that restriction, this Agreement will be binding on, inure to, and be enforceable against the parties and their respective successors and assigns. We may perform any of our obligations or exercise any of our rights under this Agreement through one or more of our Affiliates. Our failure to enforce your strict performance of any provision of this Agreement will not constitute a waiver of our right to enforce such provision or any other provision of this Agreement subsequently.

We have the right in our sole discretion to determine the content, appearance, design, functionality and all other aspects of the Services, including by redesigning, modifying, removing, or restricting access to any of them.

Because Amazon is not your agent (except for the limited purpose set out in the Transaction Processing Service Terms (if the Elected Country for a Service is the United States)), or the customer's agent for any purpose, Amazon will not act as either party's agent in connection with resolving any disputes between participants related to or arising out of any transaction.

We will send all notices and other communications regarding this Agreement to you at the e-mail addresses you designated for notifications and updates in your program application or within Seller Central, or by any other means then specified by Amazon. We may also communicate with you electronically and in other media, and you consent to such communications regardless of any "E-mail Preferences" (or similar preferences or requests) you may have indicated on the applicable Amazon Site, on Seller Central, or by any other means. You may change your e-mail addresses and certain other information in Seller Central. You will ensure that all of your information is up to date and accurate at all times. You must send all notices and other communications relating to Amazon to our Merchant Services Team by using the Contact Us form.

This Agreement incorporates and you accept the applicable Service Terms and Program Policies, which Amazon may modify from time to time. If any provision of this Agreement is deemed unlawful, void, or for any reason unenforceable, then that provision will be deemed severable from these terms and conditions and will not affect the validity and enforceability of any remaining provisions. If the Elected Country is Canada, then it is the express wish of the parties that this Agreement and the applicable Service Terms and Program Policies have been drafted in English. (The following is a French translation of the preceding sentence: Si le pays de service est le Canada, les parties conviennent que la présente autorisation et tous les termes et conditions applicables s'y rattachant soient rédigés en anglais.) If the Elected Country is any country other than Japan, we may make available translations to this Agreement and the applicable Service Terms and Program Policies, but the English version will control. This Agreement represents the entire agreement between the parties with respect to the Services and related subject matter and supersedes any previous or contemporaneous oral or written agreements and understandings.

DEFINITIONS

As used in this Agreement, the following terms have the following meanings:

"Affiliate" means, with respect to any entity, any other entity that directly or indirectly controls, is controlled by, or is under common control with that entity.

"Amazon Associated Properties" means any website or other online point of presence, mobile application, service or feature, other than an Amazon Site, through which any Amazon Site, any Webstore Site, or products or services available on any of them, are syndicated, offered, merchandised, advertised or described.

"Amazon Contracting Party" means the party outlined below.

- If the Elected Country is Canada:

Service	Amazon Contracting Party
Selling on Amazon	Amazon Services International, Inc.
Selling on Amazon (if your account is enabled to list Optional Coverage Plans)	Amazon Services Contracts, Inc.
Fulfillment by Amazon	Amazon.com.ca, Inc.
Amazon Clicks	Amazon Services International, Inc.

- If the Elected Country is Japan:

Service	Amazon Contracting Party
Selling on Amazon	Amazon Services International, Inc.
Fulfillment by Amazon	Amazon Japan Logistics K.K.
Amazon Clicks	Amazon Services International, Inc.

- If the Elected Country is Mexico:

Service	Amazon Contracting Party
Selling on Amazon	Servicios Comerciales Amazon México S. de R.L. de C.V.
Fulfillment by Amazon	Servicios Comerciales Amazon México S. de R.L. de C.V.

- If the Elected Country is the United States:

Service	Amazon Contracting Party
Selling on Amazon	Amazon Services LLC
Selling on Amazon (if your account is enabled to list Optional Coverage Plans)	Amazon Services Contracts, Inc.
Fulfillment by Amazon	Amazon Services LLC
Amazon Webstore	Amazon Services LLC
Amazon Clicks	Amazon Services LLC
Transaction Processing Services	Amazon Payments, Inc., provided that if you registered for or used a Service prior to June 30, 2014, then Amazon Services LLC may in its discretion perform the Transaction Processing Services

"Amazon Site" means, as applicable, the CA Amazon Site, the JP Amazon Site, the MX Amazon Site, or the US Amazon Site.

"Amazon Transaction Information" means, collectively, Order Information and any other data or information acquired by you or your Affiliates from Amazon, its Affiliates, or otherwise as a result of this Agreement, the transactions contemplated by this Agreement, or the parties' performance under this Agreement.

"CA Amazon Site" means the website, the primary home page of which is identified by the url www.amazon.ca, and any successor or replacement of such website.

"Content" means copyrightable works under applicable Law.

"Excluded Products" means the items described on the applicable Restricted Products pages in Seller Central, any other applicable Program Policy, or any other information made available to you by Amazon.

"Governing Courts" means the applicable one of the following:

- the state or Federal court in King County, Washington (if the Elected Country is Canada, Mexico or the United States),
- Tokyo District Court or Tokyo Summary Court depending upon the amount of the claim made (if the Elected Country is Japan).

"Governing Laws" means the applicable one of the following:

- the laws of the State of Washington, United States together with the Federal Arbitration Act and other applicable federal law (if the Elected Country is Canada, Mexico or the United States),
- the laws of Japan (if the Elected Country is Japan).

"Insurance Limits" means the applicable one of the following:

- One Million Canadian Dollars ($1,000,000) (if the Elected Country is Canada),
- One Hundred Million Japanese Yen (¥100,000,000) (if the Elected Country is Japan),
- Ten Million Mexican Pesos ($10,000,000) (if the Elected Country is Mexico),

- One Million U.S. Dollars ($1,000,000) (if the Elected Country is the United States).

"Insurance Threshold" means the applicable one of the following:

- Ten Thousand Canadian Dollars ($10,000) (if the Elected Country is Canada),
- One Million Japanese Yen (¥1,000,000) (if the Elected Country is Japan),
- One Hundred Thousand Mexican Pesos ($100,000) (if the Elected Country is Mexico),
- Ten Thousand U.S. Dollars ($10,000) (if the Elected Country is the United States).

"Intellectual Property Right" means any patent, copyright, Trademark, domain name, moral right, trade secret right, or any other intellectual property right arising under any Laws and all ancillary and related rights, including all rights of registration and renewal and causes of action for violation, misappropriation or infringement of any of the foregoing.

"JP Amazon Site" means that website, the primary home page of which is identified by the url www.amazon.co.jp, and any successor or replacement of such website.

"Law" means any law, ordinance, rule, regulation, order, license, permit, judgment, decision or other requirement, now or in the future in effect, of any governmental authority (e.g. on a federal, state, or provincial level, as applicable) of competent jurisdiction.

"Local Currency" means the applicable one of the following:

- U.S. Dollars (if the Elected Country is the United States),
- Canadian Dollars (if the Elected Country is Canada),
- Mexican Pesos (if the Elected Country is Mexico),
- Japanese Yen (if the Elected Country is Japan).

"MX Amazon Site" means the website, the primary home page of which is identified by the url www.amazon.com.mx, and any successor or replacement of such website.

"Optional Coverage Plans" means warranties, extended service plans and related offerings, in each case as determined by us, that you offer.

"Order Information" means, with respect to any of Your Products ordered through an Amazon Site or a Webstore Site, the order information and shipping information that we provide or make available to you.

"Person" means any individual, corporation, partnership, limited liability company, governmental authority, association, joint venture, division or other cognizable entity, whether or not having distinct legal existence.

"Program Policies" means all terms, conditions, policies, guidelines, rules and other information on the applicable Amazon Site or on Seller Central, including those shown on the "Policies and Agreements" section of Seller Central or elsewhere in the "Help" section of Seller Central (and, for purposes of the Fulfillment by Amazon Service, specifically including the FBA Guidelines). All Program Policies applicable to Webstore by Amazon also apply to Amazon Webstore, unless otherwise specifically stated.

"Promotion Site" means that ecommerce website, the primary home page of which is identified by the URL www.sellername.amazonwebstore.com, in which "sellername" is a name representing you that we elect to include in such URL.

"Sales Proceeds" means the gross proceeds from any of Your Transactions, including all shipping and handling, gift wrap and other charges, and including taxes and customs duties to the extent specified in the applicable Tax Policies.

"Seller Central" means the online portal and tools made available by Amazon to you, for your use in managing your orders, inventory and presence on a particular Amazon Site, a Webstore Site, or any other online point of presence.

"Service" means each of the following services: Selling on Amazon, Amazon Webstore, Fulfillment by Amazon, Amazon Clicks (including Amazon Product Ads, Amazon Sponsored Products and Amazon Text Ads), and, if the Elected Country for a Service is the United States, the Transaction Processing Services, together in each case with any related services and materials we make available.

"Service Terms" means the service terms applicable to each Service, which are made part of this Agreement upon the date you elect to register for or use the applicable Service, and any subsequent modifications we make to those terms.

"Technology" means any: (a) ideas, procedures, processes, systems, methods of operation, concepts, principles and discoveries protected or protectable under the

Laws of any jurisdiction; (b) interfaces, protocols, glossaries, libraries, structured XML formats, specifications, grammars, data formats, or other similar materials; and (c) software, hardware, code, technology or other functional item.

"Trademark" means any trademark, service mark, trade dress (including any proprietary "look and feel"), trade name, other proprietary logo or insignia or any other source or business identifier, protected or protectable under any Laws.

"US Amazon Site" means that website, the primary home page of which is identified by the url www.amazon.com, and any successor or replacement of such website.

"Webstore Service" has the meaning described in the Webstore Service Terms.

"Webstore Site" has the meaning described in the Webstore Service Terms.

"Your Materials" means all Technology, Your Trademarks, Content, Your Product information, data, materials, and other items or information provided or made available by you or your Affiliates to Amazon or its Affiliates.

"Your Personnel" means any third party warranting, administering or otherwise involved in the offer, sale, performance or fulfillment of Your Products, including any of your employees, representatives, agents, contractors, or subcontractors.

"Your Product" means any product or service (including Optional Coverage Plans) that: (a) you offer through the Webstore Service or the Selling on Amazon Service; (b) is made available for advertising by you through the Amazon Clicks Service; or (c) is fulfilled or otherwise processed through the Fulfillment by Amazon Service.

"Your Sales Channels" means all sales channels and other means through which you or any of your Affiliates offers products or services, other than physical stores.

"Your Taxes" means any and all sales, goods and services, use, excise, premium, import, export, value added, consumption and other taxes, regulatory fees, levies (specifically including environmental levies) or charges and duties assessed, incurred or required to be collected or paid for any reason (a) in connection with any advertisement, offer or sale of products or services by you on or through or in connection with the Services; (b) in connection with any products or services provided for which Your Products are, directly or indirectly, involved as a form of payment or exchange; or (c) otherwise in connection with any action, inaction or omission of you or your Affiliates, or any Persons providing products or services, or your or their respective employees, agents, contractors or representatives, for which Your Products are, directly or indirectly, involved as a form of payment or exchange. Also, if the Elected Country is the United States, Mexico or Canada, as it is used in the Fulfillment by Amazon Service Terms, this defined term also means any of the types of taxes, duties, levies or fees mentioned above that are imposed on or collectible by Amazon or any of its Affiliates in connection with or as a result of fulfillment services including the storage of inventory or packaging of Your Products and other materials owned by you and stored by Amazon, shipping, gift wrapping or other actions by Amazon in relation to Your Products pursuant to the Fulfillment by Amazon Service Terms.

"Your Trademarks" means Trademarks of yours that you provide to us: (a) in non-text form for branding purposes; and (b) separate from (and not embedded or otherwise incorporated in) any product specific information or materials.

"Your Transaction" means any sale of Your Product(s) through an Amazon Site or any Webstore Site.

SELLING ON AMAZON SERVICE TERMS

The Selling on Amazon Service (**"Selling on Amazon"**) is a Service that allows you to offer certain products and services directly on the Amazon Sites (which, if the Elected Country is the United States, includes a Promotion Site that we may make available from time to time during the Term and on which certain of Your Products may be offered).

These Selling on Amazon Service Terms are part of the Agreement, but, unless specifically provided otherwise, concern and apply only to your participation in Selling on Amazon. BY REGISTERING FOR OR USING THE SELLING ON AMAZON SERVICE, YOU (ON BEHALF OF YOURSELF OR THE BUSINESS YOU REPRESENT) AGREE TO BE BOUND BY THE AGREEMENT, INCLUDING THESE SELLING ON AMAZON SERVICE TERMS. **NOTWITHSTANDING THE PREVIOUS SENTENCE, IF YOU HAVE ENTERED INTO A SEPARATE AGREEMENT THAT PERMITS YOU TO OFFER YOUR PRODUCTS THROUGH A PARTICULAR AMAZON SITE (E.G., A MERCHANTS@ AMAZON.COM PROGRAM AGREEMENT, MERCHANTS @ AMAZON.CO.JP PROGRAM AGREEMENT OR ANY PREDECESSOR OF THOSE AGREEMENTS), THEN TO THE EXTENT THAT YOU CONTINUE TO LIST AND SELL YOUR PRODUCTS ON THAT AMAZON SITE PURSUANT TO SUCH SEPARATE AGREEMENT, TRANSACTIONS OF YOUR PRODUCTS ON THAT AMAZON SITE AND ANY TAX SERVICES WE MAKE AVAILABLE UNDER THAT AGREEMENT ARE**

GOVERNED BY THE TERMS OF THAT AGREEMENT AND NOT BY THESE SELLING ON AMAZON SERVICE TERMS.

S-1 Your Product Listings and Orders.

S-1.1 Products and Product Information. You will provide in the format we require accurate and complete Required Product Information for each product or service that you offer through any Amazon Site and promptly update that information as necessary to ensure it at all times remains accurate and complete. You will also ensure that Your Materials, Your Products (including packaging) and your offer and subsequent sale of any of the same on any Amazon Site comply with all applicable Laws (including all minimum age, marking and labeling requirements) and do not contain any sexually explicit (except to the extent expressly permitted under our applicable Program Policies), defamatory or obscene materials. You may not provide any information for, or otherwise seek to offer any Excluded Products on any Amazon Sites; or provide any URL Marks for use, or request that any URL Marks be used, on any Amazon Site.

S-1.2 Product Listing; Merchandising; Order Processing. We will enable you to list Your Products on a particular Amazon Site, and conduct merchandising and promote Your Products as permitted by us (including via the Amazon Associated Properties or any other functions, features, advertising, or programs on or in connection with the applicable Amazon Site). We may use mechanisms that rate, or allow shoppers to rate, Your Products and your performance as a seller and Amazon may make these ratings and feedback publicly available. We will provide Order Information to you for each order of Your Products through the applicable Amazon Site. We will also receive all Sales Proceeds on your behalf for each of these transactions and will have exclusive rights to do so, and will remit them to you in accordance with these Selling on Amazon Service Terms.

S-1.3 Shipping and Handling Charges. For Your Products ordered by customers on or through an Amazon Site that are not fulfilled using Fulfillment by Amazon, you will determine the shipping and handling charges subject to our Program Policies and standard functionality (including any category-based shipping and handling charges we determine, such as for products offered by sellers on the Individual selling plan and BMVD Products generally). When we determine the shipping and handling charges, you will accept them as payment in full for your shipping and handling. Please refer to the Fulfillment by Amazon Service Terms for Your Products that are fulfilled using Fulfillment by Amazon.

S-1.4 Credit Card Fraud. We will bear the risk of credit card fraud (i.e., a fraudulent purchase arising from the theft and unauthorized use of a third party's credit card information) occurring in connection with Your Transactions except in connection with Seller-Fulfilled Products that are not fulfilled strictly in accordance with the Order Information and Shipment Information. You will bear all other risk of fraud or loss. We may in our sole discretion withhold for investigation, refuse to process, restrict shipping destinations for, stop and/or cancel any of Your Transactions. You will stop or cancel orders of Your Products if we ask you to do so. If you have already transferred Your Products to a carrier or shipper when we ask you to stop or cancel an order, you will use commercially reasonable efforts to stop or cancel delivery of that order. You will refund any customer (in accordance with Section S-2.2) that has been charged for an order that we stop or cancel.

S-2 Sale and Fulfillment: Refunds and Returns.

S-2.1 Sale and Fulfillment. Other than as described in the Fulfillment by Amazon Service Terms for each Amazon Site for which you register or use the Selling on Amazon Service, you will: (a) source, offer, sell and fulfill your Seller-Fulfilled Products, and source and, offer and sell your Amazon-Fulfilled Products, in each case in accordance with the terms of the applicable Order Information, this Agreement, and all terms provided by you or us and displayed on the applicable Amazon Site at the time of the order and be solely responsible for and bear all risk for those activities; (b) package each of Your Products in a commercially reasonable manner complying with all applicable packaging and labeling requirements and ship each of Your Products on or before its Expected Ship Date; (c) retrieve Order Information at least once each business day; (d) only cancel Your Transactions as permitted pursuant to your terms and conditions appearing on the applicable Amazon Site at the time of the applicable order or as may be required under this Agreement; (e) fulfill Your Products throughout the Elected Country (except to the extent prohibited by Law or this Agreement); (f) provide to Amazon information regarding fulfillment and order status and tracking (to the extent available), in each case as requested by us using the processes designated by us, and we may make any of this information publicly available; (g) comply with all Street Date instructions; (h) ensure that you are the seller of each of Your Products; (i) include an order-specific packing slip, and, if applicable, any tax invoices, within each shipment of Your Products; (j) identify yourself as the seller of each of Your Products on all packing slips or other information included or provided in connection with Your Products and as the Person to which a customer may return the applicable product; and (k) except as expressly permitted by this Agreement, not send customers emails confirming orders or fulfillment of Your Products. If any of Your Products are fulfilled using Fulfillment by Amazon, the Fulfillment by Amazon Service Terms for the applicable Amazon Site will apply to the storage, fulfillment and delivery of such Amazon-Fulfilled Products.

S-2.2 Cancellations, Returns and Refunds. For all of Your Products that are not fulfilled using Fulfillment by Amazon, you will accept and process cancellations, returns, refunds and adjustments in accordance with this Agreement and the Amazon Refund Policies for the applicable Amazon Site published at the time of the applicable order, and we may inform customers that these policies apply to Your Products. Except as otherwise described in the Program Policies, you will determine and calculate the amount of all refunds and adjustments (including any taxes, shipping and handling or other charges) or other amounts to be paid by you to customers in connection with Your Transactions, using functionality we enable for your account. This functionality may be modified or discontinued by us at any time without notice. You will route all payments to customers in connection with Your Transactions through Amazon. We will provide those payments to the customer (which may be in the same payment form originally used to purchase Your Product or as otherwise determined by us), and you will reimburse us for all amounts we pay. For all of Your Products that are fulfilled using Fulfillment by Amazon, the Amazon Refund Policies for the applicable Amazon Site published at the time of the applicable order will apply and you will comply with them. You will promptly provide refunds and adjustments that you are obligated to provide under the applicable Amazon Refund Policies and as required by Law, and in no case later than thirty (30) days after the obligation arises.

S-3 Problems with Your Products.

S-3.1 Delivery Errors and Nonconformities; Recalls. You are solely responsible for any non-performance, non-delivery, misdelivery, theft or other mistake or act in connection with the fulfillment of Your Products, except to the extent caused by: (a) credit card fraud for which we are responsible under Section S-1.4; or (b) our failure to make available to you Order Information as it was received by us or resulting from address verification. Notwithstanding the previous sentence, for those of Your Products that are fulfilled using Fulfillment by Amazon, if any, the Fulfillment by Amazon Service Terms for the applicable Amazon Site will apply to non-delivery, misdelivery, theft or other mistake or act in connection with the fulfillment of those of Your Products. You are also responsible for any non-conformity or defect in, or any public or private recall of, any of Your Products or other products provided in connection with Your Products. You will notify us promptly as soon as you have knowledge of any public or private recalls of Your Products or other products provided in connection with Your Products.

S-3.2 A-to-z Guarantee and Chargebacks. If we inform you that we have received a claim under the "A-to-z Guarantee" offered on a particular Amazon Site, or any chargeback or other dispute, concerning one of Your Transactions, you will deliver to us in a format and manner we specify: (a) proof of fulfillment of Your Product(s) (as applicable); (b) the applicable Amazon order identification number; (c) a description of Your Product(s) (as applicable); and (d) any terms provided by you or us and displayed on the Amazon Site at the time of the transaction in question. If you fail to comply with the prior sentence, or if the claim, chargeback, or dispute is not caused by: (i) credit card fraud for which we are responsible under Section S-1.4; or (ii) our failure to make your Order Information available as the same was received by us or resulting from address verification, then you will promptly reimburse us in accordance with the Service Fee Payments section of this Agreement for the amount of the customer purchase (including the Purchase Price, all associated shipping and handling charges and all taxes, but excluding any associated Referral Fees retained and not subject to refund by Amazon) and all associated credit card association, bank or other payment processing, re-presentment and/or penalty fees associated with the original purchase and any chargeback or refund, in each case to the extent paid or payable by us or our Affiliates. If the Elected Country is Japan and we receive a claim under the

"A-to-z Guarantee" concerning one of Your Transactions and we determine that we are responsible for that claim then we will purchase the returned products from the customer.

S-4 Parity with Your Sales Channels.

Subject to this Section S-4, you are free to determine which of Your Products you wish to offer on a particular Amazon Site. You will maintain parity between the products you offer through Your Sales Channels and the products you list on any Amazon Site by ensuring that : (a) the Purchase Price and every other term of offer or sale of Your Product (including associated shipping and handling charges, Shipment Information, any "low price" guarantee, rebate or discount, any free or discounted products or other benefit available as a result of purchasing one or more other products, and terms of applicable cancellation, return and refund policies) is at least as favorable to Amazon Site users as the most favorable terms upon which a product is offered or sold via Your Sales Channels (excluding consideration of Excluded Offers); (b) customer service for Your Products is at least as responsive and available and offers at least the same level of support as the most favorable customer services offered in connection with any of Your Sales Channels (this requirement does not apply to customer service for payment-related issues on Your Transactions, which we will provide); and (c) the Content, product and service information and other information under Section S-1.1 regarding Your Products that you provide to us is of at least the same level of quality as the highest quality information displayed or used in Your Sales Channels. If you become aware of any non-compliance with (a) above, you will promptly compensate adversely affected customers by making appropriate refunds to them in accordance with Section S-2.2. For Amazon-Fulfilled Products, if the shipping and handling charges associated with the sale and fulfillment of any of Your Products offered on an Amazon Site are included (and not separately stated) in the item price listed for Your Product (collectively a **"Shipping Inclusive Purchase Price"**), then the parity obligation in (a) above will be satisfied if the Shipping Inclusive Purchase Price and each other term of offer or sale for the product on the Amazon Site are at least as favorable to Amazon Site users as the purchase price and each other term of offer or sale for the product (including any and all separately stated shipping and handling charges) pursuant to which the product or service is offered or sold via any of Your Sales Channels.

S-5 Compensation.

You will pay us: (a) the applicable Referral Fees; (b) any applicable Variable Closing Fee; (c) the non-refundable Selling on Amazon Subscription Fee in advance each month; and (d) any other applicable fees described in this Agreement (including any applicable Program Policies). **"Selling on Amazon Subscription Fee"** means the fee specified as such on the Selling on Amazon Fee Schedule for the applicable Amazon Site at the time such fee is payable. With respect to each of Your Transactions: (i) **"Sales Proceeds" has the meaning set out in this Agreement**; (ii) "Variable Closing Fee" means the applicable fee, if any, as specified on the Variable Closing Fee Schedule for the applicable Amazon Site; and (iii) **"Referral Fee"** means the applicable fee based on the Sales Proceeds from Your Transaction through the applicable Amazon Site specified on the Selling on Amazon Fee Schedule for that Amazon Site at the time of Your Transaction, based on the categorization by Amazon of the type of product that is the subject of Your Transaction; provided, however, that Sales Proceeds will not include any shipping charges set by us in each of the following two cases: (y) in the case of Your Transactions that consist solely of products fulfilled using Fulfillment by Amazon; and (z) in the case of Media Products.

S-6 Remittance of Sales Proceeds & Refunds.

Except as otherwise stated in this Agreement, we will remit to you on a bi-weekly (14 day) (or at our option, more frequent) basis, which may vary for each Elected Country, any Sales Proceeds received by us or our Affiliates but not previously remitted to you as of the date that is two (2) business days prior to the date of remittance (the **"Remittance Calculation Date"**) (which you will accept as payment in full for Your Transactions), less: (a) the Referral Fees; (b) the applicable Variable Closing Fee; (c) any Selling on Amazon Subscription Fees; and (d) any other applicable fees described in this Agreement (including any applicable Program Policies). When you either initially provide or later change Your Bank Account information, the Remittance Calculation Date may be deferred by up to 14 days. You will not have the ability to initiate or cause payments to be remitted to you. For sellers that registered after October 30, 2011 and are on the Individual selling plan, the remittance amount will not include Sales Proceeds from the 14-day period before the date of remittance. If you refund money to a customer in connection with one of Your Transactions, and the refund is routed through us (or our Affiliate), on the next available Remittance Calculation Date we will refund to you the amount of the Referral Fee paid by you to us attributable to the amount of the customer refund (including refunded taxes and customs duties only to the extent specified in the applicable Tax Policies), less the Refund Administration Fee for each of Your Products refunded that is not a BMVD Product, which amount we may retain as an administrative fee; provided, however, that in the case of a complete refund of Sales Proceeds for a Media Product, we will refund to you the full amount of any Variable Closing Fee paid by you to us (and in the case of a partial refund of Sales Proceeds for a Media Product, we will not refund to you any portion of any Variable Closing Fee paid by you to us). We will remit any amounts to be refunded by us pursuant to this subsection from time to time together with the next remittance to be made by us to you. **"Refund Administration Fee"** means the applicable fee described on the Refund Administration Fee Schedule for the applicable Amazon Site.

S-7 Control of Amazon Sites.

We have the right in our sole discretion to determine the content, appearance, design, functionality and all other aspects of the Amazon Sites, including by redesigning, modifying, removing or restricting access to any of them, and by suspending, prohibiting or removing any listing.

S-8 Effect of Termination.

Upon termination of these Selling on Amazon Service Terms in connection with a particular Amazon Site, all rights and obligations of the Parties under these Selling on Amazon Service Terms with regard to such Amazon Site will be extinguished, except that the rights and obligations of the Parties with respect to Your Transactions occurring during the Term will survive the termination or expiration of the Term.

SELLING ON AMAZON DEFINITIONS

"Amazon-Fulfilled Products" means any of Your Products that are fulfilled using the Fulfillment by Amazon Service.

"Amazon Refund Policies" means the return and refund policies published on the applicable Amazon Site and applicable to products and services offered via that Amazon Site.

"BMVD Product" means any book, magazine or other publication, sound recording, video recording, and/or other media product in any format, including any subscription, in each case excluding any software product, computer game, and/or video game.

"Excluded Offer" means any discount, rebate, promotional offer, or other term of offer and/or sale that you: (a) have attempted to make available through a particular Amazon Site but that we do not honor or support (but only until such time as we honor or support the same on such Amazon Site); or (b) make available solely to Third Parties that either (i) purchase products solely for resale and who are not end users of such products (i.e., wholesale purchasers), or (ii) if the Elected Country is Canada, Mexico, or the United States have affirmatively elected and opted-in to participate in your or one of your Affiliates' membership-based customer loyalty or customer incentive programs.

"Expected Ship Date" means, with respect to any of Your Products, either: (a) the end of the shipping availability period (which begins as of the date on which the relevant order is placed by the customer), or the shipping availability date, as applicable, specified by you in the relevant inventory/product data feed for Your Product; or (b) if you do not specify shipping availability information in such inventory/product data feed or that Your Product is in a product category that Amazon designates as requiring shipment within two (2) business days, two (2) business days after the date on which the relevant order is placed by the customer.

"Media Product" means any book, magazine or other publication, sound recording, video recording, software product, computer game, videogame, or other media product in any format, including any related subscription, offered through an Amazon Site.

"Purchase Price" means the total amount payable or paid for Your Product (including taxes and shipping and handling charges only to the extent specified in the applicable Tax Policies).

"Remittance Calculation Date" is defined in <u>Section S-6</u>.

"Required Product Information" means, with respect to each of Your Products in connection with a particular Amazon Site, the following (except to the extent expressly not required under the applicable Program Policies): (a) description, including as applicable, location-specific availability and options, scheduling guidelines and service cancellation policies; (b) SKU and UPC/EAN/JAN numbers, and other identifying information as Amazon may reasonably request; (c) information regarding in-stock status and availability, shipping limitations or requirements, and Shipment Information (in each case, in accordance with any categorizations prescribed by Amazon from time to time); (d) categorization within each Amazon product category and browse structure as prescribed by Amazon from time to time; (e) digitized image that accurately depicts only Your Product, complies with all Amazon image guidelines, and does not include any additional logos, text or other markings; (f) Purchase Price; (g) shipping and handling charge (in accordance with our standard functionality); (h) any text, disclaimers, warnings, notices, labels, warranties or other content required by applicable Law to be displayed in connection with the offer, merchandising, advertising or sale of Your Product; (i) any vendor requirements, restocking fees or other terms and conditions applicable to such product that a customer should be aware of prior to purchasing the product; (j) brand; (k) model; (l) product dimensions; (m) weight; (n) a delimited list of technical specifications; (o) SKU and UPC/EAN/JAN numbers (and other identifying information as we may reasonably request) for accessories related to Your Product that is available in our catalog; (p) the state or country Your Product ships from; and (q) any other information reasonably requested by us (e.g., the condition of used or refurbished products).

"**Seller-Fulfilled Products**" means any of Your Products that are not fulfilled using the Fulfillment by Amazon Service.

"**Shipment Information**" means, with respect to any of Your Products, the estimated or promised shipment and delivery date.

"**Street Date**" means the date(s), if any, specified by the manufacturer, distributor and/or licensor of a product as the date before which specified information regarding such product (e.g., title of a book) should not be disclosed publicly, or such product should not be delivered or otherwise made available to customers.

"**URL Marks**" means any Trademark, or any other logo, name, phrase, identifier or character string, that contains or incorporates any top level domain (e.g., .com, .edu, .ca, .fr, .jp) or any variation of a top level domain (e.g., dot com, dotcom, net, or com).

"**Your Transaction**" is defined in the General Terms of this Agreement; however, as used in these Selling on Amazon Service Terms, it means any and all such transactions through Selling on Amazon only.

WEBSTORE SERVICE TERMS

Amazon Webstore (which, for purposes of this Agreement, includes Webstore by Amazon, unless specifically stated otherwise) (the **"Webstore Service"**) provides access to and use of an e-commerce website through which you can offer and sell Your Products (a **"Webstore Site"**). The Webstore Service is not currently available in Canada, Mexico or Japan.

These Webstore Service Terms are part of this Agreement, and, unless specifically provided otherwise, concern and apply only to your participation in the Webstore Service. BY REGISTERING FOR OR USING THE WEBSTORE SERVICE, YOU (ON BEHALF OF YOURSELF OR THE BUSINESS YOU REPRESENT) AGREE TO BE BOUND BY THE AGREEMENT, INCLUDING THESE WEBSTORE SERVICE TERMS.

W-1 Listing and Promotion.

Each sale of Your Products through your Webstore Site is a sale by you. You will determine what is for sale on your Webstore Site, but you may not list any product on the Webstore Site that is an Excluded Product. You will ensure that you list all of Your Products in accordance with this Agreement, including any applicable Program Policies.

W-2 Information.

You will provide in the format we require accurate and complete Webstore Required Product Information and all other information requested by us to process payments for you and to otherwise operate your Webstore Site. You will update such information as necessary to ensure it at all times remains accurate and complete. If you provide us with any images of Your Product, you will, unless we otherwise agree, first remove any logos, text or other marking included on the image except for any logos, text or other marking that actually appears on the product. You will either: (a) upload to us the "shipping confirmation files" as required by us, including all shipment notification, shipping status and order tracking information requested by us from time to time, and any other information as requested by us to process payments based on Your Product shipment status; provided, that if you are using Fulfillment by Amazon to fulfill any of your customer orders, the Fulfillment by Amazon Service Terms will apply with respect to such orders; or (b) use the Manage Your Orders tool in Seller

Central to manage and upload the required "shipping confirmation files" from Seller Central. We may provide this shipment and payment related information to users of the Webstore Site. We will make available certain information and reports relating to Your Transactions as we determine and have no obligation to make available any other information. We may use mechanisms that rate, or may allow users to rate, your performance as a seller, and may post those ratings and feedback on the Webstore Site or any Amazon Site or otherwise make it publicly available. Any use on your Webstore Site of content displayed on an Amazon Site, or links to an Amazon Site, will be subject to the terms of the Amazon Associates Operating Agreement.

W-3 Your Product Transactions.

W-3.1 General; Sale and Fulfillment. You will be solely responsible for, and bear all risk and liability for, sourcing, storing, selling, and fulfilling all of Your Products. As such, you are responsible for any non-conformity or defects in, damage to, or theft of or claims regarding the delivery or non-delivery of Your Products. You will handle such responsibilities, and agree to complete transactions for the items that you have listed in accordance with these Webstore Service Terms and applicable Program Policies. Notwithstanding anything in this Section W-3.1, for those of Your Products that are fulfilled using Fulfillment by Amazon (if any), the Fulfillment by Amazon Service Terms will apply to our storage, fulfillment and delivery of Your Products. All sales of Your Products on or through the Webstore Site will be final and may not be cancelled or revoked by you except pursuant to the applicable terms and conditions that appear on the Webstore Site.

W-3.2 Order and Payment Processing. We will process all payments, refunds and adjustments for Your Transactions. Amazon's, or one of its Affiliates', name will appear on the customer's credit card statement (which may also display, at our option, your name). We will determine the time at which we process payments, refunds and adjustments for Your Transactions in our sole discretion. However, you are always the seller of record. We may withhold for investigation, or refuse to process, any of Your Transactions. We do not need to accept any particular form of order or payment for Your Product, or honor or accept any discounts, coupons, gift certificates, or other offers or incentives made available by you. We may in our sole discretion withhold for investigation or to refuse to process any transaction involving Your Products or any other products or services on or through the Webstore Site. We may use the services of one or more third party, processors or financial institutions in connection with the Webstore Service (each, a "Processor"). If total Sales Proceeds from Your Transactions exceed $20,000 per month for any three consecutive months, you agree to the additional terms and conditions between you and the Processor(s) as provided in the Credit Card Association Agreement. If you have entered into a separate agreement with one of our Affiliates that governs order and payment processing in connection with Your Transactions, you will be subject to the terms of that agreement notwithstanding anything to the contrary in this Agreement.

W-3.3 Fraud and Order Stops/Cancellations. We will bear the risk of credit card fraud (i.e. fraudulent purchases arising from the theft and unauthorized use of a third party's credit card information) occurring in connection with Your Transactions, except with respect to Your Transactions that you do not fulfill in accordance with the Order Information made available to you by us (including shipping Your Product only to the recipient and at the shipping address specified in the Order Information made available by Amazon), and you will bear all other risk of fraud or loss. You will promptly inform us of any changes to the product mix of Your Products or any pattern of fraudulent or other improper activities with respect to any of Your Product(s) that has resulted or may result in a higher incidence of fraud or other impropriety associated with transactions involving it (or them) than other similar products. You will stop or cancel orders of Your Products if we so direct (and if the customer has already been charged, you will execute the refunds for these orders) and will provide to us telephone and email contact information for a designated contact available during business hours whom we can contact regarding fraud, order stops and cancellations and similar concerns, who will cooperate with us and who has access and ability promptly to cancel or stop orders from being shipped. We may restrict destinations to which you may ship Your Products sold on or through any Webstore Site.

W-3.4 Refunds and Returns. Except for those of Your Products, if any, that are fulfilled using Fulfillment by Amazon (in which case the Fulfillment by Amazon Service Terms will apply), you will accept and process returns of, and (using the functionality we make available to you) provide refunds and adjustments for, Your Products in accordance with these Webstore Service Terms and your policies posted on the Webstore Site at the time of the applicable sale, and you will calculate and refund any associated taxes required to be refunded. You will route all refund (and adjustment) payments through Amazon or its designated Affiliate. Amazon or its designated Affiliate will credit the applicable customer account, and you will reimburse Amazon for all amounts so credited. The functionality we make available to you for processing returns and adjustments may be modified or discontinued by us at any time without notice and is subject to the terms of this Agreement. Except for those of Your Products, if any, that are fulfilled using Fulfillment by Amazon (in which case the Fulfillment by Amazon Service Terms will apply), we have no obligation to accept any returns of any of Your Products.

W-3.5 Delivery Errors and Nonconformities; Product Recalls. You are responsible for any non-delivery, misdelivery, theft or other mistake or act in connection with the fulfillment of Your Products, except to the extent caused by (a) credit card fraud for which we are responsible under Section W-3.3; or (b) our failure to make available to you Order Information as it was received by us or resulting from address verification. Notwithstanding the previous sentence, for those of Your Products that are fulfilled using Fulfillment by Amazon (if any), the Fulfillment by Amazon Service Terms will apply to non-delivery, misdelivery, theft or other mistake or act in connection with the fulfillment of those of Your Products. You are also responsible for any non-conformity or defect in, or any public or private recall of, any of Your Products. You will notify us promptly as soon as you have knowledge of any public or private recalls of Your Products.

W-3.6 A-to-z Guarantee and Chargebacks. If we inform you that we have received a claim under the "A-to-z Guarantee" (or any substantially consistent offer), or any chargeback or other dispute, concerning one of Your Transactions, you will deliver to us within seven (7) days: (a) proof of delivery of the applicable Your Product(s); (b) the applicable Amazon order identification number; and (c) a description of the applicable Your Product(s). If you fail to comply with the prior sentence, or if the claim, chargeback, or dispute is not caused by (i) credit card fraud for which we are responsible under Section W-3.3, or (ii) our failure to make your Order Information available as the same was received by us or resulting from address verification, then you will promptly reimburse us for the amount of the customer purchase (including the Purchase Price, all associated shipping and handling charges and all taxes) and all associated credit card association, bank or other payment processing, re-presentment and/or penalty fees associated with the original purchase and any chargeback or refund, in each case to the extent paid or payable by us or our Affiliates. We may require that you establish a separate reserve account (a "**Reserve**") to secure the performance of your payment obligations under this Agreement, in an amount as determined by us. Without limiting the foregoing, we may require a Reserve if you have a high rate of chargebacks, refunds, or other indicia of performance problems related to your use of the Webstore Service. The Reserve will be in an amount as determined by us to cover anticipated chargebacks or credit risk based on your processing history or such amount designated by our Processor(s) and the Reserves will be subject to the Transaction Processing Service Terms (if the Elected Country for a Service is the United States).

W-4 Customer Service.

W-4.1 General. The provisions in this Section W-4 apply only in connection with sales of Your Products through the Webstore Site that are not fulfilled using Fulfillment by Amazon. For customer service obligations pertaining to orders of Your Products using the Selling on Amazon Service or orders of Your Products fulfilled using Fulfillment by Amazon, the Service Terms applicable to those Services will apply. You will refer customer issues to us according to the responsibilities below, in a timely, professional and courteous manner and at the applicable "Contact Us" form, email address and/or phone number provided for such purpose by us. You will not establish direct phone or email transfer functionality of customer service contacts to us, forward customer emails to us, or disclose our customer service contact information unless in response to a customer contact concerning a customer service issue for which we are responsible under these Webstore Service Terms.

    W-4.2 Our Customer Service Responsibilities. As between you and us, we will be solely responsible for all customer service issues relating to payment, credit card processing, debiting or crediting, and the "A-to-z Guarantee".

    W-4.3 Your Customer Service Responsibilities. Unless provided otherwise elsewhere in these Webstore Service Terms, you will be solely responsible for all customer service issues relating to Your Products (including pricing, rebates, item information, availability, technical support, functionality and warranty), Your Product order fulfillment and shipping and handling, Your Product order cancellation by you or any customer, returns, refunds and adjustments, and feedback concerning experiences with your personnel, policies or processes. In performing customer service, you will always present yourself as a separate entity from us.

W-5 Data and Communications. We and you will co-own all the Customer Account Information and Webstore Transaction Information. Neither you nor we will need to pay any royalties or account to the other in connection with your or our use of any Customer Account Information or Webstore Transaction Information. You and your Affiliates will: (a) at all times comply with all Laws, including any Law related to the use of this type of information; and (b) comply with any applicable policies posted on the Webstore Site regarding use of this transaction and customer data. We are not liable for protection or privacy of electronic mail or other information transferred through the Internet or any other network you or your customers may utilize, including without limitation in connection with the provision of the Webstore Service; or the back up of any of your files or data.

W-6 Pricing and Remittance.

W-6.1 Your Product Pricing and Terms of Sale Generally. You are free to determine the price for each of Your Products listed for sale on your Webstore Site.

W-6.2 Shipping & Handling Charges. You will determine shipping and handling charges for Your Products sold on or through the Webstore Site, but will comply with any shipping and handling charge Program Policies. If Your Product is fulfilled using Fulfillment by Amazon, this section will not apply and the Fulfillment by Amazon Service Terms will apply.

W-6.3 Remittance and Compensation.

W-6.3.1 Fees. You will pay us: (a) applicable Webstore Referral Fees; and (b) the applicable non-refundable Webstore Subscription Fee(s) in advance for each month of the term of this Agreement. **"Webstore Subscription Fee"** means the applicable fee(s) specified on the Webstore Fee Schedule at the time such fee is payable. With respect to each of Your Transactions: (i) **"Sales Proceeds"** has the meaning set out in the General Terms of this Agreement; and (ii) **"Webstore Referral Fee"** means the applicable percentage of Sales Proceeds from Your Transaction through the Webstore Site specified on the Webstore Fee Schedule at the time of Your Transaction.

W-6.3.2 Remittance of Sales Proceeds. We will remit to you on a bi-weekly (14-day) (or at our option, more frequent) basis any Webstore Sales Proceeds received by us but not previously remitted to you as of the date that is two (2) business days prior to the date of remittance (the **"Remittance Calculation Date"**), less: (a) the Webstore Referral Fees due for such sums; and (b) any Webstore Subscription Fees due. You will accept our remittances under the previous sentence as payment in full for the sale and shipping and handling of Your Products.

W-6.3.3 Refunds. If you refund money to a customer in connection with Your Transaction, and the refund is routed through us, we will refund to you the amount of the Webstore Referral Fee paid by you to us attributable to the amount of the customer refund (excluding any refunded taxes), less the lower of (a) five dollars ($5); or (b) twenty percent (20%) of the Webstore Referral Fee, which we may retain as an administrative fee. We will remit any amounts to be refunded by us under this subsection from time to time together with the next remittance to be made by us to you pursuant to subsection W-6.3.1 above.

W-7 Provision and Use of the Webstore Service.

W-7.1 License to the Webstore Service and Amazon Materials. Subject to this Agreement (including, but not limited to, Section W-7.2 (License Restrictions) and Section W-7.5 (Messaging), we grant you a limited, revocable, non-sublicenseable, non-assignable, non-exclusive and royalty-free license to: (a) access and use the Webstore Service and the Amazon Materials in the manner permitted by this Agreement; (b) install, copy, and use any Amazon Materials we may provide, solely in conjunction with your access to and use and operation of your Webstore Site; (c) use the Amazon Marks solely in conjunction with your use and operation of your Webstore Site and solely in accordance with the Trademark Usage Guidelines; and (d) enable the access to and use of your Webstore Site by customers.

W-7.2 License Restrictions. You may not and may not authorize any other party to do the following to or with the Webstore Service, the Webstore Site or the Amazon Materials: (a) reverse engineer, decompile, or disassemble them; (b) modify or create derivative works based upon them in whole or in part; (c) distribute copies of them; (d) remove any proprietary notices or labels on them; (e) use any Public Software in any manner that requires, pursuant to the license applicable to such Public Software, that the Webstore Service or any Amazon Materials be disclosed, licensed, distributed or otherwise made available to anyone; or (f) resell, lease, rent, transfer, sublicense, or otherwise transfer rights to them. In addition to any other rights or remedies that we may have, any use in violation of this section will immediately terminate your right to use the Webstore Service, the Webstore Site, the Amazon Materials, and the Amazon Marks.

W-7.3 Ownership; Reservation of Rights. You acknowledge and agree that we (or our licensors, as applicable) own all right, title and interest in and to the Webstore Service, the Amazon Materials, and Amazon Marks, and, except as explicitly included in this Agreement, you do not, by virtue of this Agreement or otherwise, acquire any ownership interest or rights in or to the Webstore Service, the Amazon Materials, any Amazon Marks, or any other intellectual property or technology that we provide or use in connection with the Webstore Service. All licenses not expressly granted in these Webstore Service Terms are reserved and no other licenses, immunity or rights, express or implied are granted by us, by implication, estoppels or otherwise.

W-7.4 URLs.

W-7.4.1 General. Except as provided in Section W-7.4.2, you will be responsible for securing all rights to the URL(s) for the Webstore Site, including maintaining the registration for the URLs with your domain name registrars. You will comply with our requirements regarding the URL(s) and its administration with the registrar so that we can provide the Webstore Service to you. You represent and warrant that the URLs used in connection with the Webstore Site does not violate any intellectual property rights or any other proprietary rights of any person. Except in connection with any URL provided by us as described in Section W-7.4.2, you will not include "amazon", or any other Amazon Mark or any variation or similar misspelling in any URL used in connection with the Webstore Site, or otherwise.

W-7.4.2 Amazon Provided URL. We may provide you with a URL to use in connection with your Webstore Site. If you choose to use it you will comply with our requirements for its administration.

W-7.5 Messaging. We will have the right to determine the use of any Amazon Marks and any messaging or notice on the Webstore Site, for example, we will control how our role in processing orders and payments is explained to the customer, and (if applicable) how our "A-to-z Guarantee" is described. The Webstore Site will also display privacy and customer account use and creation messaging, which will include any terms we may require. At a minimum, you will ensure that your privacy policy discloses that you use third party service providers to provide your Webstore Site and that your third party service providers will have access to customer information. Should we allow or require you to include any Amazon Marks or messaging, you will do so strictly in accordance with instructions we provide to you.

W-8 Effect of Termination.

Upon any termination of the term of this Agreement or these Webstore Service Terms, all rights and obligations of the parties under these Webstore Service Terms will terminate, except that: the rights and obligations of the parties under Sections W-2, W-3, W-4, W-5, W-6 and W-8 with respect to Your Transactions occurring prior to termination will survive such termination. Upon any termination of the term of this Agreement or these Webstore Service Terms, you will immediately cease and discontinue all use of the Amazon Marks.

W-9 Miscellaneous.

Your Representations; Compliance with Laws. In addition to your representation and warranties in Section 5 of the General Terms of this Agreement, you represent and warrant to us that: (a) all of Your Products and their packaging comply and will comply with all applicable marking and labeling requirements required by law; (b) none of Your Products are or will be produced or manufactured, in whole or in part, by child labor or by convict or forced labor; (c) you and all of your subcontractors, agents and suppliers involved in producing or delivering Your Products will strictly adhere to all applicable Laws of the Elected Country, its territories and all other countries where Your Products are produced or delivered, regarding the operation of their facilities and their business and labor practices, including without limitation working conditions, wages, hours and minimum ages of workers; (d) you will not, unless we otherwise agree, redirect any customers or prospective customers from the Webstore Site to any other sales channel, and will not use the Webstore Service for any purpose other than the offer or sale of Your Products as contemplated in this Agreement; (e) Your Materials, Your Products and your offer and subsequent sale of any of the same complies with all applicable Laws (including all marking and labeling requirements) and do not contain any defamatory, obscene or sexually explicit materials (except to the extent expressly permitted under applicable Program Policies); (f) you will ensure that Your Transactions are made at no less than fair value under the antidumping laws of the United States and will otherwise comply with the antidumping laws of the United States, its territories and of all other countries where Your Products are produced, delivered, or intended to be sold; (g) in connection with the Webstore Service or your Webstore Site, you will not separately ask for or require any customers or prospective customers to provide any credit card, debit card, bank account, or other information related to a payment method; and (h) you will not, without our prior consent, use any third party payment service for the processing of payments for transactions associated with your Webstore Site.

WEBSTORE DEFINITIONS

"Amazon Functionality" means all techniques, know-how, features and functionality specific to development of a website presence to display products loaded into the Amazon platform, including the following features and functions: search, browse, product detail display, shopping cart and credit card transaction processing, order/account lookup, and storefront administration & merchandising.

"Amazon Mark" is defined in the Trademark Usage Guidelines.

"Amazon Materials" means: (a) the Amazon Functionality (including, without limitation, all related techniques, know-how, algorithms, materials, specifications and source code); and (b) all Webstore Service-related product information, APIs, and any distinctive trade dress and trade styles (including, without limitation, color schemes), proprietary fonts, and the design, formatting, organization and structure of screens and other elements included within the Webstore Site.

"Amazon Product" means any products that are sold and fulfilled by Amazon (or one of its Affiliates) on its own behalf.

"Amazon Transaction" means the sale of any Amazon Product through the Webstore Site for which Amazon (or its Affiliate) receives Amazon Transaction Revenues.

"Amazon Transaction Revenues" means: (a) the aggregate revenues (excluding taxes, bad debt, gift-wrapping charges, shipping and handling charges, or services charges and credit card processing fees) derived by Amazon and its Affiliates from sales of Amazon Products through the Webstore Site as provided in this Agreement; less (b) any revenues attributable to returned Amazon Products, if such revenues previously were included in "Amazon Transaction Revenues".

"Customer Account Information" means the following non-transaction-specific information you receive from Amazon prior to the expiration or termination of this Agreement with respect to customer accounts created or otherwise used to purchase Your Products on the Webstore Site: customer name, physical address, e-mail address and phone numbers. Notwithstanding the foregoing and for the avoidance of doubt, Customer Account Information does not include: (a) any Webstore Transaction Information; (b) any credit card, other account or identifying number of, or any other information specifically concerning, any payment instrument or method; (c) sign-in credentials; (d) information that pertains specifically to functionality of the Webstore Site (e.g., personalization settings); or (e) user clickstream information.

"Public Software" means any software, documentation or other material that contains, or is derived (in whole or in part) from, any software, documentation or other material that is distributed as free software, open source software (e.g., Linux) or similar licensing or distribution models, including, but not limited to software, documentation or other material licensed or distributed under any of the following licenses or distribution models, or licenses or distribution models similar to any of the following: (a) the GNU General Public License (GPL); Lesser/Library GPL (LGPL), or Free Documentation License; (b) The Artistic License (e.g., PERL); (c) the Mozilla Public License; (d) the Netscape Public License; (e) the Sun Community Source License (SCSL); (f) the Sun Industry Standards License (SISL); (g) the BSD License; and (h) the Apache License.

"Shipment Information" means, with respect to any of Your Products, the estimated or promised shipment and/or delivery date.

"Webstore Required Product Information" means with respect to each of Your Products, the following: (a) a description of Your Product; (b) the UPC code (unless we otherwise agree), SKU number for Your Product, and any other identifying information about Your Product that we request; (c) information regarding the in-stock status, shipping availability period or shipping availability date, and Your shipping limitations or requirements (in each case, in accordance with any categorizations we prescribe from time to time); (d) the categorization of Your Product within each applicable Amazon browse structure that we prescribe from time to time; (e) a digitized image of Your Product (provided that you will first remove any logos, text or other marking included on such image except to the extent that such logos, text or other marking actually appear on Your Product); (f) the price for Your Product; (g) any text, disclaimers, warnings, notices, labels or other content required by applicable law to be displayed in connection with the offer, merchandising, advertising or sale of Your Product; (h) any vendor requirements, restocking fees or other terms and conditions applicable to such product that a customer should be aware of prior to purchasing the product; (i) brand; (j) model; (k) product dimensions; (l) weight; (m) a delimited list of technical specifications; (n) UPC code and SKU number (and other identifying information as Amazon may reasonably request) for accessories related to Your Product that are available in Amazon's catalog; and (o) any other information we reasonably request (e.g., the condition of used or refurbished products).

"**Webstore Transaction Information**" means the following information you receive from Amazon associated with any orders of Your Product through your Webstore Site: total transaction amount; order ID#; order item code; SKU; product name; quantity; price; and adjustments. Notwithstanding the foregoing and for the avoidance of doubt, Webstore Transaction Information does not include: (a) any Customer Account Information; (b) sign-in credentials; (c) user click-stream information; or (d) any credit card or other account or identifying number of, or any other information specifically concerning, any payment instrument or method.

FULFILLMENT BY AMAZON SERVICE TERMS

Fulfillment by Amazon ("**FBA**") provides fulfillment and associated services for Your Products.

These FBA Service Terms are part of the Agreement, and, unless specifically provided otherwise, concern and apply only to your participation in FBA. BY REGISTERING FOR OR USING FBA, YOU (ON BEHALF OF YOURSELF OR THE BUSINESS YOU REPRESENT) AGREE TO BE BOUND BY THE AGREEMENT, INCLUDING THESE FBA SERVICE TERMS. You expressly agree that Amazon may engage its Affiliate(s) or a third party in order to complete one or more of the fulfillment and associated services outlined below.

If the Elected Country is Japan, the following applies to you: Notwithstanding anything to the contrary in the Agreement, if there should be any subject matter specified in the "Standard Storage Bailment Terms and Conditions (Hyoujun Soko Kitaku Yakkan – Otsu)" that is not specified in the Agreement, including these FBA Service Terms, upon your request, such provision will be determined by discussion and mutual agreement of the parties.

FULFILLMENT SERVICES

F-1 Your Products

Once you are accepted into FBA, you must apply to register each product you offer that you wish to include in the FBA program. We may refuse registration in FBA of any product, including on the basis that it is an FBA Excluded Product or that it violates applicable Program Policies. You may at any time withdraw registration of any of Your Products from FBA.

F-2 Product and Shipping Information

You will, in accordance with applicable Program Policies, provide in the format we require accurate and complete information about Your Products registered in FBA, and will provide Fulfillment Requests for any Units fulfilled using FBA that are not sold through an Amazon Site (**"Multi-Channel Fulfillment Units"**). You will promptly update any information about Your Products in accordance with our requirements and as necessary so that the information is at all times accurate and complete.

F-3 Shipping to Amazon

F-3.1 Except as otherwise provided in Section F-3.4 and Section F-5, FBA is limited to Units that are shipped to and from fulfillment centers located within the applicable Elected Country, to be delivered to customers in the same Elected Country only. You will ship Units to us in accordance with applicable Program Policies. You will be responsible for all costs incurred to ship the Units to the shipping destination (including costs of freight and transit insurance) and Amazon will not pay any shipping costs except as provided in Section F-3.2. You are responsible for payment of all customs, duties, taxes and other charges. In the case of any improperly packaged or labeled

Unit, we may return the Unit to you at your expense (pursuant to <u>Section F-7</u>) or re-package or re-label the Unit and charge you an administrative fee.

F-3.2 You will not deliver to us, and we may refuse to accept, any shipment or Unsuitable Unit. We may return or dispose of any Unsuitable Unit as provided in <u>Section F-7</u> (and you will be deemed to have consented to such action): (a) immediately if we determine in our sole discretion that the Unit creates a safety, health or liability risk to Amazon, our personnel or any third party; (b) if you fail to direct us to return or dispose of any Unsuitable Unit within thirty (30) days after we notify you that the Unit has been recalled; or (c) except as otherwise provided in this <u>Section F-3.2</u>, if you fail to direct us to return or dispose of any Unsuitable Unit within ninety (90) days after we notify you that we are in possession of it. In addition, you will reimburse us for any expenses we incur in connection with any Unsuitable Units.

F-3.3 If the Elected Country is the United States or Mexico, we may, at our option, allow you to ship Units at your expense (as described in <u>Section F-9.2</u>) to fulfillment centers using discounted shipping rates that we may make available to you for certain carriers. In such event, you will use the processes and supply the information that we require for you to obtain such discounted rates. You also must comply with standard operating procedures, weight and size restrictions, and other shipping requirements of the applicable carriers. If we provide you with the estimated shipping costs prior to shipment, you acknowledge and agree that actual shipping costs may vary from such estimates. In addition, if the weight of the Unit, as determined by the applicable carrier, differs from that submitted by you to us for purposes of determining the estimated shipping costs, then: (a) you may be charged more than the estimated shipping costs if the carrier determines that such Unit weighs more than as submitted by you; or (b) you may be charged the full amount of the estimated shipping costs even if the carrier determines the weight to be less than that submitted by you. You will not use our carrier account information (e.g., carrier account number, amount of shipping rates, etc.) for any purpose, nor disclose such information to any third party, and you will protect such information as Amazon's confidential information in accordance with Section 11 of the General Terms of this Agreement. As between you, us and our carrier, you will be the shipper of record, and we will be the payer of record with respect to all Units shipped to us using such discounted rates. Title and risk of loss for any Unit shipped using discounted rates provided by us under this Section will remain with you, and our provision of such shipping rates will not create any liability or responsibility for us with respect to any delay, damage or loss incurred during shipment. You authorize the applicable carrier to provide us with all shipment tracking information.

F-3.4 If you ship Units from outside the applicable Elected Country to fulfillment centers, you will list yourself as the importer/consignee and nominate a customs broker. If Amazon is listed on any import documentation, Amazon reserves the right to refuse to accept the Units covered by the import documents and any costs assessed against or incurred by Amazon will be collected from Your Bank Account, deducted from amounts payable to you, or by other method at our election.

F-4 Storage

We will provide storage services as described in these FBA Service Terms once we confirm receipt of delivery. We will keep electronic records that track inventory of Units by identifying the number of Units stored in any fulfillment center. We will not be required to physically mark or segregate Units from other inventory units (e.g., products with the same Amazon standard identification number) owned by us, our Affiliates or third parties in the applicable fulfillment center(s). If we elect to commingle Units with such other inventory units, both parties agree that our records will be sufficient to identify which products are Units. We may move Units among facilities. If there is a loss of or damage to any Units while they are being stored, we will, as your sole remedy, reimburse you in accordance with the FBA Guidelines, and you will, at our request, provide us a valid tax invoice for the compensation paid to you. If we reimburse you for a Unit, we will be entitled to dispose of the Unit pursuant to Section F-7. This reimbursement is our total liability for any duties or obligations that we or our agents or representatives may have as a bailee or warehouseman, and your only right or remedy that you may have as a bailor. At all other times, you will be solely responsible for any loss of, or damage to, any Units. Our confirmed receipt of delivery does not: (a) indicate or imply that any Unit has been delivered free of loss or damage, or that any loss or damage to any Unit later discovered occurred after confirmed receipt of delivery; (b) indicate or imply that we actually received the number of Units of Your Product(s) specified by you for such shipment; or (c) waive, limit or reduce any of our rights under this Agreement. We reserve the right to impose, and change from time to time, scheduling restrictions and volume limitations on the delivery and storage of your inventory in fulfillment centers, and you will comply with any of these restrictions or limitations.

F-5 Fulfillment

As part of our fulfillment services, we will ship Units from our inventory of Your Products to the shipping addresses in the Elected Country included in valid customer orders, or submitted by you as part of a Fulfillment Request. We may ship Units together with products purchased from other merchants, including any of our Affiliates. We also may ship Units separately that are included in a single Fulfillment Request. If you elect to participate in our export fulfillment services, we will also ship Your Products that we determine to be eligible (each, a **"Foreign-Eligible Product"**) to Foreign Addresses within countries we determine to be eligible for foreign shipments, subject to the additional terms on foreign shipments in the applicable FBA Guidelines.

F-6 Customer Returns

F-6.1 You will be responsible for and will accept and process returns of, and provide refunds and adjustments for, any Multi-Channel Fulfillment Units in accordance with the Agreement (including the applicable Program Policies).

F-6.2 We will receive and process returns of any Amazon Fulfillment Units that were shipped to addresses within the Elected Country in accordance with the terms of your Seller Agreement, these FBA Service Terms and the Program Policies. Any Sellable Units that are also Amazon Fulfillment Units and that are properly returned will be placed back into the inventory of Your Products in the FBA Program. We may fulfill customer orders for Your Products with any returned Amazon Fulfillment Units. Except as provided in Section F-7, you will retake title of all Units that are returned by customers.

F-6.3 Except as provided in Section F-5, we will, at your direction, either return or dispose of any Selling on Amazon Unit that is returned to us and that we determine is an Unsuitable Unit as provided in Section F-7. Without limitation of our rights under Section F-7.1, we may elect to return or dispose of that Unsuitable Unit as provided in Section F-7, and you will be deemed to have consented to our election if you fail to direct us to return or dispose of the Unsuitable Unit within ninety (90) days after we notify you of the Unsuitable Unit.

F-6.4 If Amazon receives a customer return of a Multi-Channel Fulfillment Unit, you will direct us to return or dispose of the Unit at your own cost failing which we may dispose of the Unit as provided in <u>Section F-7</u>.

F-7 Returns to You and Disposal

F-7.1 You may, at any time, request that Units be returned to you. We may return Units to you for any reason, including upon termination of these FBA Service Terms. These returned shipments will be sent to your designated shipping address that is within the Elected Country (or, at Amazon's sole discretion, your designated shipping address). If the address we have for you is outdated, incorrect or outside the Elected Country, or if we cannot make arrangements for you to pay for the return shipment, the Unit(s) will be deemed abandoned and we may elect to dispose of the Unit(s) as provided in this Agreement.

F-7.2 You may, at any time, request that we dispose of Units. We may dispose of any Unit we are entitled to dispose of in the manner we prefer. Title to each disposed Unit will transfer to us at no cost to us as necessary for us to dispose of the Unit, and we will retain all proceeds, if any, received from the disposal of any Unit.

F-7.3 You will promptly notify us of any recalls or threatened recalls of any of Your Products and cooperate and assist us in connection with any recalls, including by initiating the procedures for returning items to you under our standard processes. You will be responsible for all costs and expenses you, we or any of our or your Affiliates incur in connection with any recall or threatened recall of any of Your Products (including the costs to return, store, repair, liquidate or deliver to you or any vendor any of these products).

F-8 Customer Service

F-8.1 For Multi-Channel Fulfillment Units we will have no customer service obligations other than to pass any inquiries to your attention at the contact you provide, and to make available a reasonable amount of information regarding the status of the fulfillment of Your Products if you request it and if and to the extent we possess the requested information. You will ensure that all of your policies and messaging to your customers regarding shipping of Your Products and other fulfillment-related matters, reflect our policies and requirements, including with regard to shipping methods, returns and customer service; and, you will conspicuously display on your website(s), in emails or in other media or communications any specific disclosures, messaging, notices, and policies we require.

F-8.2 We will be responsible for and have sole discretion regarding all customer service issues relating to packaging, handling and shipment and customer returns, refunds and adjustments related to Amazon Fulfillment Units. We will have the right to determine whether a customer will receive a refund, adjustment or replacement for any Amazon Fulfillment Unit and to require you to reimburse us where we determine you have responsibility in accordance with the Agreement (including these FBA Service Terms and the Program Policies). Except as provided in this Section F-8 regarding any Amazon Fulfillment Units, customer service will be handled in accordance with your Seller Agreement.

F-8.3 In situations relating to Amazon Fulfillment Units where the wrong item was delivered or the item was damaged or lost or is missing, unless we determine that the basis for such request is caused by you or any of your employees, agents or contractors, we will, as your sole and exclusive remedy and at our option: (a) for any Amazon Fulfillment Unit, (i) ship a replacement Unit to the customer and reimburse you in accordance with the FBA Guidelines for the replacement Unit, or (ii) process a refund to the customer and reimburse you in accordance with the FBA Guidelines for the Unit; or (b) for any Multi-Channel Fulfillment Unit, reimburse you in accordance with the FBA Guidelines for the Unit (and you will, at our request, provide us a valid tax invoice for the compensation paid to you). Any customer refund will be processed in accordance with the Selling on Amazon and the Transaction Processing Service Terms (if the Elected Country for a Service is the United States). Notwithstanding the Selling on Amazon Service Terms, we will be entitled to retain the applicable fees payable to us under the Selling on Amazon Service Terms and these FBA Service Terms, respectively. Except as expressly provided in this Section F-8.3, you will be responsible for all costs associated with any replacement or return.

F-8.4 If we provide a replacement Unit or refund as described in Section F-8.3 to a customer and that customer returns the original Unit to us, we will be entitled to dispose of the Unit pursuant to Section F-7, or, if it is a Sellable Unit, we may, at our option, place such Unit back into your inventory in accordance with Section F-6. If we do put a Unit back into your inventory, you will reimburse us for the applicable Replacement Value (as described in the FBA Guidelines) of the returned Unit. Any replacement Unit shipped by us under these FBA Service Terms will be deemed to be, and will be treated in the same manner as, an order and sale of such Unit from you to the customer via the applicable Amazon Site or Service in accordance with, and subject to, the terms and conditions of this Agreement and your Seller Agreement.

F-9 Compensation for Fulfillment Services

F-9.1 Handling and Storage Fees. You will pay us the applicable fees described in the applicable Fulfillment by Amazon Fee Schedule. You will be charged the Storage Fees beginning on the day (up to midnight) that the Unit arrives at a fulfillment center and is available for fulfillment by Amazon (or in the case of any Unsuitable Unit, the arrival day (up to midnight)), until the earlier of: (a) the day (up to midnight) we receive a valid customer order for such product or a request from you to return or dispose of the Unit; or (b) the day (up to midnight) we actually ship the Unit to your designated return location or dispose of the Unit.

F-9.2 Shipping and Gift Wrap. For any Amazon Fulfillment Units we will determine the amounts charged to the customer for shipping and gift wrap services for the Units that we fulfill through the FBA Program. As between you and us, these charges will be your charges to the customer, and we will report them to you. We will charge you (and you will pay us) a fee equal to the amount of such charges to the customer. In the case of shipments of Units sold through the Amazon Site that qualify for the "Free Shipping" promotion, the amounts charged to the customer for shipping the Selling on Amazon Units that Amazon fulfills will first be charged to the customer and will next be deducted from the total charges to the customer as your promotion and Amazon will not charge you the fee described above. If the Elected Country is the United States and you ship Units to us using the shipping rates that we may make available pursuant to Section F-3.3, you will reimburse us for the actual amounts charged to us by the applicable carrier for such shipments.

F-9.3 Proceeds. We may keep all proceeds of any Units that we dispose of or to which title transfers, including returned, damaged or abandoned Units. You will have no security interest, lien or other claim to the proceeds that we receive in connection with the sale, fulfillment and/or shipment of these Units.

F-10 Indemnity

In addition to your obligations under Section 6 of the General Terms of this Agreement, you also agree to indemnify, defend and hold harmless us, our Affiliates, and our and their respective officers, directors, employees, representatives and agents against any Claim that arises from or relates to: (a) the Units (whether or not title has transferred to us, and including any Unit that we identify as yours pursuant to Section F-4 regardless of whether such Unit is the actual item you originally sent to us), including any personal injury, death or property damage; (b) the shipment, export or delivery of Your Products to Foreign Addresses (including with respect to any classification data and other information provided by you to us in connection therewith, and notwithstanding any rights we have under Section F-5 or any certifications we may make in connection with the shipment, export or delivery of Your Products); (c) any of Your Taxes or the collection, payment or failure to collect or pay Your Taxes; and, if applicable (d) any sales, use, value added, personal property, gross receipts, excise, franchise, business or other taxes or fees, or any customs, duties or similar assessments (including penalties, fines or interest on any of the foregoing) imposed by any government or other taxing authority in connection with the shipment of Foreign-Eligible Products to Foreign Addresses (collectively, **"Foreign Shipment Taxes"**).

F-11 Release

You, on behalf of yourself and any successors, subsidiaries, Affiliates, officers, directors, shareholders, employees, assigns and any other person or entity claiming by, through, under or in concert with them (collectively, the **"Releasing Parties"**), irrevocably acknowledge full and complete satisfaction of and unconditionally and irrevocably release and forever fully discharge Amazon and each of our Affiliates, and any and all of our and their predecessors, successors, and Affiliates, past and present, as well as each of our and their partners, officers, directors, shareholders, agents, employees, representatives, attorneys, and assigns, past and present, and each of them and all Persons acting by, through, under or in concert with any of them (collectively, the **"Released Parties"**), from any and all claims, obligations, demands, causes of action, suits, damages, losses, debts or rights of any kind or nature, whether known or unknown, suspected or unsuspected, absolute or contingent, accrued or unaccrued, determined or speculative (collectively, **"Losses"**) which the Releasing Parties now own or hold or at any time have owned or held or in the future may hold or own against the Released Parties, or any of them, arising out of, resulting from, or in any way related to the shipment, export or delivery of Your Products to Foreign Addresses, including any tax registration or collection obligations. You, on behalf of yourself and all other Releasing Parties, recognize that you, and each of them, may have some Losses, whether in tort, product liability, contract, warranty or otherwise, against the Released Parties of which you, or any of them, are totally unaware and unsuspecting, or which may arise or accrue after the date you register for or use FBA, which the Releasing Parties are giving up by agreeing to these FBA Service Terms. It is your intention in agreeing to these FBA Service Terms that these FBA Service Terms will deprive the Releasing Parties of each and all such Losses and prevent the Releasing Party from asserting any such Losses against the Released Parties, or any of them. In addition to the foregoing, you acknowledge, on behalf of yourself and all other Releasing Parties that you are familiar with Section 1542 of the Civil Code of the State of California, as follows:

"A general release does not extend to claims which the creditor does not know or suspect to exist in his favor at the time of executing the release, which if known by him must have materially affected his settlement with the debtor."

You, on behalf of yourself and all other Releasing Parties, expressly waive and relinquish any rights that you had or may have under Section 1542 of the Civil Code of the State of California or any similar provision of the law of any other jurisdiction, to the full extent that you may lawfully waive all such rights pertaining to the subject matter of these FBA Service Terms.

F-12 Disclaimer

IN ADDITION TO THE DISCLAIMER IN SECTION 7 OF THE GENERAL TERMS OF THIS AGREEMENT, WE DISCLAIM ANY DUTIES OF A BAILEE OR WAREHOUSEMAN, AND YOU WAIVE ALL RIGHTS AND REMEDIES OF A BAILOR (WHETHER ARISING UNDER COMMON LAW OR STATUTE OR OTHERWISE), RELATED TO OR ARISING OUT OF ANY POSSESSION, STORAGE OR SHIPMENT OF YOUR PRODUCTS BY US OR OUR AFFILIATES OR ANY OF OUR OR THEIR CONTRACTORS OR AGENTS.

F-13 Effect of Termination

Following any termination of the Agreement or these FBA Service Terms in connection with a particular Elected Country, we will, as directed by you, return to you or dispose of the Units held in that Elected Country as provided in Section F-7. If you fail to direct us to return or dispose of the Units within ninety (90) days after termination, then we may elect to return and/or dispose of the Units in whole or in part, as provided in Section F-7, and you will be deemed to have consented to this. Upon any termination of these FBA Service Terms in connection with a particular Elected Country, all rights and obligations of the parties under these FBA Service Terms in connection with such Elected Country will be extinguished, except that the rights and obligations of the parties under Sections F-1, F-2, F-3, F-4, F-5, F-6, F-7, F-8, F-9, F-11, F-12 and F-13 with respect to Units received or stored by Amazon as of the date of termination will survive the termination.

F-14 Tax Matters

You understand and acknowledge that storing Units at fulfillment centers may create tax nexus for you in any country, state, province, or other localities in which your Units are stored, and you will be solely responsible for any taxes owed as a result of such storage. If any Foreign Shipment Taxes or Your Taxes are assessed against us as a result of performing services for you in connection with the FBA Program or otherwise pursuant to these FBA Service Terms, you will be responsible for such Foreign Shipment Taxes and Your Taxes and you will indemnify and hold Amazon harmless from such Foreign Shipment Taxes and Your Taxes as provided in Section F-10 of these FBA Service Terms.

F-15 Additional Representation

In addition to your representations and warranties in Section 5 of the General Terms of this Agreement, you represent and warrant to us that: (a) you have valid legal title to all Units and all necessary rights to distribute the Units and to perform under these FBA Service Terms; (b) you will deliver all Units to us in new condition (or in such condition otherwise described by you in the applicable Your Product listing) and in a merchantable condition; (c) all Units and their packaging will comply with all applicable marking, labeling and other requirements required by Law; (d) no Unit is or will be produced or manufactured, in whole or in part, by child labor or by convict or forced labor; (e) you and all of your subcontractors, agents and suppliers involved in producing or delivering Units will strictly adhere to all applicable Laws of the Elected Country, its territories and all other countries where Units are produced or delivered, regarding the operation of their facilities and their business and labor practices, including working conditions, wages, hours and minimum ages of workers; and (f) that all Foreign-Eligible Products (i) can be lawfully exported from Canada, Mexico, Japan, or the United States, as applicable, without any license or other authorization; and (ii) can be lawfully imported into, and comply with all applicable Laws of, any eligible country.

FBA DEFINITIONS

"Amazon Fulfillment Units" means Units fulfilled using FBA that are sold through an Amazon Site. For avoidance of doubt, if you have successfully registered for or used both the FBA and Selling on Amazon Services, then the term "Amazon Fulfillment Units" and the defined term "Amazon Fulfilled Products" in the Selling on Amazon Service Terms both refer to the same items.

"FBA Excluded Product" means any Unit that is an Excluded Product, or is otherwise prohibited by the applicable Program Policies.

"Foreign Address" means (a) if the Elected Country is the United States, any mailing address that is not (i) within the fifty states of the United States or Puerto Rico, or (ii) an APO/FPO address; and (b) if the Elected Country is not the United States, any mailing address that is not within the Elected Country.

"Fulfillment Request" means a request that you submit to us (in accordance with the standard methods for submission prescribed by us) to fulfill one or more Multi-Channel Fulfillment Units.

"Multi-Channel Fulfillment Units" has the meaning in Section F-2.

"Sellable Unit" means a Unit that is not an Unsuitable Unit.

"Seller Agreement" means the Selling on Amazon Service Terms, the Merchants@ Program Agreement, the Marketplace Participation Agreement, any successor to any of these agreements, or any other similar agreement (as determined by Amazon) between you and us that permits you to offer products and services via a particular Amazon Site.

"Shipping Information" means with respect to any purchased Unit(s), the following information: the name of the recipient, the shipping address, the quantity of Units to be shipped, and any other shipping-related information we may reasonably request.

"Unit" means a unit of Your Product that you deliver to Amazon in connection with the FBA Program.

"Unsuitable Unit" means a Unit: (a) that is defective, damaged, or lacking required label(s); (b) the labels for which were not properly registered with Amazon before shipment or do not match the product that was registered; (c) that is an FBA Excluded Product or does not comply with the Agreement (including applicable Program Policies); (d) that Amazon determines is unsellable or unfulfillable; or (e) that Amazon determines is otherwise unsuitable.

AMAZON CLICKS SERVICE TERMS

Amazon Clicks, including Amazon Product Ads, Amazon Sponsored Products and Amazon Text Ads (together **"Amazon Clicks"**), is a Service that allows you to advertise Your Products on Amazon Network Properties.

These Amazon Clicks Service Terms are part of the Agreement, and, unless specifically provided otherwise, concern and apply only to your participation in Amazon Clicks. BY REGISTERING FOR OR USING AMAZON CLICKS, YOU (ON BEHALF OF YOURSELF OR THE BUSINESS YOU REPRESENT) AGREE TO BE BOUND BY THE AGREEMENT, INCLUDING THESE AMAZON CLICKS SERVICE TERMS.

C-1 Amazon Clicks

Your Ads may be displayed or made available on Amazon Network Properties as we determine. We do not guarantee that Your Ads will be displayed or made available on any Amazon Network Property, or that Your Ads will appear in any particular position or rank. Notwithstanding any other provision of the Agreement, we may in our sole discretion restrict, modify or otherwise determine the content, appearance, design, functionality and all other aspects of Your Ads, and we may remove any of Your Ads without notice. Except to the extent expressly stated in the Agreement, you are solely responsible for all obligations, risks and other aspects pertaining to the sale of any products referred to in Your Ads, including order processing, order fulfillment, returns, refunds, recalls, misdelivery, theft, customer service, and collection of taxes. In addition, you are solely responsible for all ad content, URLs and any other information you submit to us in connection with Your Ads, and the websites and/or other properties to which Your Ads direct users (other than the Amazon Site).

We may use mechanisms that rate, or allow users to rate, Your Products and/or your performance, and we may make these ratings and feedback publicly available. We may use any means we determine necessary to review and monitor Your Ads to improve our service and ad quality.

C-2 Product Information

You will, in accordance with applicable Program Policies, provide, in the format we require, accurate and complete information for each of Your Ads. You will update this information as necessary to ensure that it is at all times accurate and complete. You will not provide any information for, or otherwise seek to advertise for sale on any Amazon Network Property, any products that are unlawful or are otherwise prohibited by applicable Program Policies.

C-3 Amazon Clicks Requirements

Using the highest industry standards, you will treat users and customers who link to your products via any of Your Ads with courtesy and respect during all stages of the buying process and resolve to our and their satisfaction in a timely and professional manner any related customer service matters we or they bring to your attention. You will ensure that Your Materials and your advertisement, offer, sale and fulfillment of Your Products comply with all applicable Laws and Program Policies. You will not, directly or indirectly, engage in any fraudulent, impermissible, inappropriate or unlawful activities in connection with your participation in Amazon Clicks, including: (a) sending multiple listings of identical products in the same feed or sending multiple feeds under different accounts; (b) generating fraudulent, repetitive or otherwise invalid clicks, impressions, queries or other interactions, whether through the use of automated applications or otherwise; (c) collecting any user information from any Amazon Network Property or retrieving, extracting, indexing or caching any portion of any Amazon website or services or the websites or services of our Affiliates, whether through the use of automated applications or otherwise; (d) targeting communications of any kind on the basis of the intended recipient being a user of any Amazon Network Property; (e) interfering with the proper working of any Amazon Network Property, Amazon Clicks or our systems; or (f) attempting to bypass any mechanism we use to detect or prevent any of the activities described in this paragraph.

C-4 Payment and Tax Matters

You will pay us the applicable fee per Click. The per Click fee will be determined solely by Amazon based on the amount you bid for each of Your Ads, consistent with any applicable product category minimums and Program Policies. You agree to pay us the applicable fees we calculate for your use of the Amazon Clicks Service in the applicable Local Currency only. In addition to any other means permitted by the Agreement, we may collect the applicable fees: (a) in accordance with the payment ladder described in the Program Policies; and (b) on a recurring monthly basis for any remaining unpaid fees accrued after the last ladder payment charged each month. If we choose to invoice you for amounts due to us under the Agreement, you will pay the invoiced amounts within 30 days of the date of the applicable invoice. We may require payment of interest at the rate of 1.5% per month or the highest legally permissible rate, whichever is lower, on all amounts not paid when due until paid in full. You will reimburse us for all fees incurred in connection with our collection of amounts payable and past due. You waive all claims related to the fees we charge (including fees based on suspected invalid Clicks on or invalid impressions of Your Ads), unless claimed within 60 days after the date charged. You understand third parties may generate impressions or Clicks on Your Ads for improper purposes and you accept this risk. Your sole and exclusive remedy for any suspected invalid impressions or Clicks is to request advertising credits within the timeframe set out above.

C-5 Effect of Termination

Upon any termination of the term of the Agreement or these Amazon Clicks Service Terms, all rights and obligations of the parties under these Amazon Clicks Service Terms will terminate, except that Sections C-1, C-2, C-4, C-5, C-6 and C-7 will survive termination.

C-6 Agents

If you are an Agent: (a) you represent and warrant that you have been appointed as an agent of an Amazon Clicks Participant, that you are duly authorized to enter into this Agreement on behalf of the Amazon Clicks Participant and have full power and authority to bind the Amazon Clicks Participant to this Agreement, and that the Agreement including these Amazon Clicks Service Terms will be enforceable against the Amazon Clicks Participant in accordance with its terms; (b) you will, upon our request, provide us written confirmation of the agency relationship between you and the Amazon Clicks Participant, including, for example, the Amazon Clicks Participant's express acknowledgment that you are its Agent and are authorized to act on its behalf in connection with Amazon Clicks; (c) except as set forth in the Agreement, you will not make any representation, warranty, promise or guarantee about Amazon Clicks, us or your relationship with us; (d) you will perform your duties pursuant to the Agreement including these Amazon Clicks Service Terms in a professional manner consistent with any requirements we may establish; (e) you will not at any time use information received in connection with Amazon Clicks to conduct any marketing efforts targeted at our existing advertisers or Amazon Clicks Participants; and (f) you and the Amazon Clicks Participant are each responsible for all payment obligations under these Amazon Clicks Service Terms, and you and the Amazon Clicks Participant each waive any rights that might require us to proceed against one or more of you prior to proceeding against the other.

C-7 Miscellaneous

C-7.1 Representations

In addition to your representations and warranties in Section 5 of the Agreement, you represent and warrant to us that: (a) on any website to which Your Ads link (other than on the Amazon Site), you will at all times post and comply with a privacy policy that complies with all applicable Laws; and (b) Your Materials and any information displayed on your website or on any website to which Your Ads link (for the Amazon Site, only to the extent such information is based on Your Materials) comply with all applicable Laws (including all marking and labelling requirements) and do not contain any false, misleading, infringing, defamatory, obscene or sexually explicit materials (except to the extent expressly permitted under applicable Program Policies).

C-7.2 Indemnification

In addition to your obligations under Section 6 of the Agreement, you agree to indemnify, defend and hold harmless us, our Affiliates, and our and their respective officers, directors, employees, representatives and agents against any Claim arising from or related to: (a) your participation in Amazon Clicks, including the display of any of Your Ads, any website, Content, data, materials or other items or information to which Your Ads link, and any actual or alleged infringement of any Intellectual Property Rights by any of the foregoing; and (b) if you are an Agent, any breach or alleged breach of your representations and warranties set forth in these Amazon Clicks Service Terms.

C-7.3 Disclaimers

IN ADDITION TO THE DISCLAIMERS IN SECTION 7 OF THE AGREEMENT, WE AND OUR AFFILIATES DISCLAIM AND YOU WAIVE ALL CLAIMS REGARDING ANY GUARANTEES ABOUT TIMING, POSITIONING, ADJACENCY, PERFORMANCE, QUANTITY OR QUALITY OF (AS APPLICABLE): PLACEMENTS, TARGETING, IMPRESSIONS, CLICKS, CLICK RATES, CONVERSION RATES, AUDIENCE SIZE, DEMOGRAPHICS OR ADVERTISING COSTS.

AMAZON CLICKS DEFINITIONS

"Agent" means an advertising agency or other person or entity who represents an Amazon Clicks Participant.

"Amazon Clicks Participant" means any person or entity enrolled in Amazon Clicks by you if you are the Agent of that person or entity.

"Amazon Network Properties" means: (a) the Amazon Site; (b) any website, device, service, feature or other online point of presence operated by Amazon or any of our Affiliates; and (c) any Amazon Associated Properties.

"Click" means each time a user clicks on any of Your Ads as determined solely by Amazon.

"Your Ads" means any advertisement for Your Product based upon Your Materials that is displayed through Amazon Clicks.

TRANSACTION PROCESSING SERVICE TERMS

BY REGISTERING FOR OR USING ANY SERVICE OTHER THAN AMAZON CLICKS FOR WHICH THE ELECTED COUNTRY IS THE UNITED STATES, YOU (ON BEHALF OF YOURSELF OR THE BUSINESS YOU REPRESENT) AGREE TO BE BOUND BY THESE TRANSACTION PROCESSING SERVICE TERMS FOR THAT SERVICE. NOTWITHSTANDING THE FOREGOING, IF A SEPARATE AGREEMENT GOVERNS THE OFFER, SALE OR FULFILLMENT OF YOUR PRODUCTS ON THE US AMAZON SITE, THE TERMS OF THAT AGREEMENT WILL CONTINUE TO GOVERN THE PROCESSING OF YOUR TRANSACTIONS TO THE EXTENT DESCRIBED IN THAT AGREEMENT.

P-1 Payments Processing Agency Appointment

You authorize Amazon Payments, Inc. ("Amazon Payments") to act as your agent for purposes of processing payments, refunds and adjustments for Your Transactions, receiving and holding Sales Proceeds on your behalf, remitting Sales Proceeds to Your Bank Account, charging your Credit Card, and paying Amazon and its Affiliates amounts you owe in accordance with this Agreement or other agreements you may have with Amazon Affiliates. Amazon Payments provides the services described in these Transaction Processing Service Terms and the related services described in Sections S-1.4, S-2.2, S-6, W-3.2, W-3.3, W-3.4, W-6.3.2, W-6.3.3, W-7.5, and F-8.3 of the Agreement (collectively, the "Transaction Processing Services").

When a buyer instructs us to pay you, you agree that the buyer authorizes and orders us to commit the buyer's payment (less any applicable fees or other amounts we may collect under this Agreement) to you. You agree that buyers satisfy their obligations to you for Your Transactions when we receive the Sales Proceeds. We will remit funds to you in accordance with this Agreement.

P-2 Remittance

Amazon Payments will remit funds to you in accordance with Sections S-6 and W-6.3.2 of the Agreement and these Transaction Processing Service Terms. Amazon Payments' obligation to remit funds collected by it on your behalf is limited to funds that have actually been received by Amazon Payments less amounts owed to Amazon, subject to chargeback or reversal or withheld for anticipated claims in accordance with this

Agreement. Without limiting Amazon's rights to collect any amounts you owe, including as described in Section 2 of the General Terms of this Agreement, Amazon Payments' receipt of Sales Proceeds discharges your obligation to pay applicable fees and other amounts under this Agreement to the extent the Sales Proceeds equal or exceed the fees and other amounts you owe and the Sales Proceeds are applied to the payment of those fees and amounts.

P-3 Your Funds

Your Sales Proceeds will be held in an account with Amazon Payments (a "Seller Account") and will represent an unsecured claim against Amazon Payments. Your Sales Proceeds are not insured by the Federal Deposit Insurance Corporation. Prior to disbursing funds to you, Amazon Payments may combine Sales Proceeds held with the funds of other users of the Services, invest them, or use them for other purposes permitted by applicable Laws. You will not receive interest or any other earnings on any Sale Proceeds. To the extent required by applicable Laws, Amazon Payments will not use any funds held on your behalf for its corporate purposes, will not voluntarily make such funds available to its creditors in the event of bankruptcy or for any other purpose, and will not knowingly permit its creditors to attach such funds.

P-4 Verification

We may at any time require you to provide any financial, business or personal information we request to verify your identity. You authorize us to obtain from time to time consumer credit reports to establish or update your Seller Account or in the event of a dispute relating to this Agreement or the activity under your Seller Account. You agree to update all Seller Account information promptly upon any change. The Amazon Payments Privacy Notice applies to your use of the Transaction Processing Services.

P-5 Dormant Accounts

If there is no activity (as determined by us) in connection with your Seller Account for the period of time set forth in applicable unclaimed property laws and we hold Sales Proceeds on your behalf, we will notify you by means designated by us and provide you the option of keeping your Seller Account open and maintaining the Sales Proceeds in your Seller Account. If you do not respond to our notice(s) within the time period we specify, we will send the Sales Proceeds in your Seller Account to your state of residency, as determined by us based on the information in your Seller Account. If we are unable to determine your state of residency or your Seller Account is associated with a foreign country, your funds may be sent to the State of Delaware.

About Cynthia Stine and Online Sales Step by Step LLC

I n addition to selling on Amazon.com for the past five years, Cynthia has also written the top-selling book *Make Thousands on Amazon in 10 Hours a Week!: How I turned $200 into $40,000 Gross Sales My First Year in Part-time Online Sales.* Her first book helped thousands of third-party sellers get started on Amazon with tight resources using the FBA program and retail arbitrage. She writes a popular blog at http://onlinesalesstepbystep.com and consults with Amazon sellers on their business issues. In 2014, her clients started turning to her to help them get reinstated from being suspended or banned.

Based on her success and experience getting people back to selling, she launched her official Reinstatement services in February 2015. She was flooded with business. The need is great, and the stakes are incredibly high. Many sellers fail when they write the appeal themselves, which can lead to them being permanently banned from selling. Cynthia has developed a system for analyzing sellers' mistakes, appealing to Amazon and – in most cases – getting her clients' businesses back up and running. It is one of the toughest and most rewarding things she's ever done.

Prior to becoming an Amazon seller, Cynthia had 25+ years business consulting and crisis management experience, which gives her a different perspective towards reinstatement. Her goal is to not only get her clients selling again, but to help them figure out how they got in trouble in the first place. She teaches them how to set up systems and put processes in place to make sure it never happens again.

When necessary, she helps sellers make changes to how they do business so they can get out of trouble and <u>stay</u> out of trouble with Amazon.

Online Sales Step by Step LLC today consists of a team of consultants in the United States and trained Amazon administrative assistants in the Philippines. While the business grew rapidly because of our reinstatement work, our mission is *Suspension Prevention*. We offer "Get Clean Stay Clean" services to act as an early warning sign to our clients. Our reinstatement and suspension prevention assessments give our clients insight into what is happening in their account right now that might make them vulnerable to suspension. Finally, we offer a wide range of custom business consulting to help our clients be better sellers.

Suspension Prevention Assessment: http://onlinesalesstepbystep.com/suspensionprevention

Reinstatement Answers & Sign-up: http://onlinesalesstepbystep.com/reinstatementfaq

Get Clean Stay Clean Services: http://onlinesalesstepbystep.com/getcleanstayclean

Blog: http://onlinesalesstepbystep.com/

Make Thousands on Amazon in 10 Hours a Week! Book: http://onlinesalesstepbystep.com/makethousandsonamazon

Phone: 214-296-0984

Get Clean Stay Clean
One Service, Many Options

Our highly skilled team can successfully manage just about any administrative aspect of your Amazon business:

* Packages customized to meet your needs
* Service levels ranging from a few hours per week to full-time employees focused on your account
* All service levels include our proprietary Canary Report, which signals issues with your Amazon business early on, giving us time to work together and solve problems
* Ongoing plans include consulting services and discounts for reinstatement services, should you ever need them

Get Clean — $250 a month

* Canary Report
* Negative feedback removal (up to 50)
* 1 call and/or email per month with consulting team
* 10% discount on reinstatement fees per month, up to 50%
* Approximately 5 hours of service per week
* Perfect for smaller Amazon accounts

Stay Clean — $500 a month

* Canary Report
* Negative feedback removal (up to 100)
* 1 call and/or email per month with consulting team
* 10% discount on our reinstatement fees per month of service up to 50% off
* 10 hours of service per week
* More advanced services for the active or growing seller

Be Squeaky Clean — $750 a month

* Canary Report
* Negative feedback removal (up to 150)
* 2 calls and/or emails per month with consulting team
* 10% discount on our reinstatement fees per month of service up to 50% off
* 15 hours of service per week
* In-depth assistance for the aggressive seller

Full Service — $1700 a month

* Canary Report
* Negative feedback removal
* 4 calls and/or emails per month with consulting team
* 1 ASIN reinstatement letter
* 10% discount on our reinstatement fees per month of service up to 50% off
* 40 hours of service per week
* Comprehensive assistance for the power seller

Additional à la carte, customized services

* Negative feedback removal
* Customer service team
* Create new listings
* Listing error repair
* Handle returns/refunds
* Manage receipts
* Shipment reconciliation
* Listing improvements/updates
* Prepare shipments
  (the online portion — work with your prep service)

Invite Cynthia Stine to speak to your group!

☞ **Suspension Prevention**
Cynthia's 15 steps you can take now to keep your Amazon seller account from being suspended.

☞ **Dirty Seller Tricks**
Ever wonder if a competitor is after you? The answer might be yes! Learn how others can manipulate the Amazon platform to get you suspended. Forewarned is forearmed!

☞ **Questions about Reinstatement**
Sellers have questions about how to get reinstated but there is a lot of confusing and conflicting information out there. Let Cynthia explain "Amazon Speak" to your members and walk them through the reinstatement process so they are empowered if they are ever suspended.

☞ **Get Clean Stay Clean**
Is your Amazon business following best practices? Cynthia shares what successful sellers do to keep their accounts clean and in good shape with Amazon.

Cynthia has worked with hundreds of Amazon sellers over the past few years and seen how their businesses get into trouble...and how they get out. Using real-world examples and case studies Cynthia shares what she has learned in order to help sellers follow best practices for their businesses.